MY DETERMINED
SPIRIT

MY DETERMINED SPIRIT

A Story of Survival

Christy Tran
with Patti Dobbe

iUniverse, Inc.
Bloomington

MY DETERMINED SPIRIT
A Story of Survival

iUniverse books may be ordered through booksellers or by contacting:

iUniverse
1663 Liberty Drive
Bloomington, IN 47403
www.iuniverse.com
1-800-Authors (1-800-288-4677)

ISBN: 978-1-4620-3993-7 (sc)
ISBN: 978-1-4620-4254-8 (ebk)

Printed in the United States of America

iUniverse rev. date: 09/23/2011

FORWARD and ACKNOWLEDGEMENTS

As my mother often told me, she came to the new world with nothing, but God had given her everything. She feels blessed to have met many wonderful people, and she only prays that God will continue to be a strong presence in her life. She and I both hope you find this book insightful. Like all wars, the Vietnam War brought an immense amount of pain, fear, and heartache. Her experience is only one of millions affected by the war, and those experiences are unavoidable. Nor should we try to avoid them: as tragic and horrific as it may seem, living despite such odds not only affects those who have survived, but also those whose lives are affected by the survivors.

My mother would like to dedicate this book to her family and thank them for their patience throughout the years.

Carolyn Tran,
on behalf of Tran Phuong Anh,
"Christy" Tran

I met Christy Tran, whom I know as Victoria, in 2001, when she became my hairdresser, after I had moved from Austin, Texas, to Amarillo, Texas. Over the years we visited while she worked to make me presentable to rest of the world. During our talks she slowly began sharing the details of her life in Vietnam during the infamous war years. I became fascinated with her story. Some of her experiences seemed unbelievable; however, the fervor with which she spoke told me it was all true. She lived a life that only a few people could truly understand. She endured the horrors of war and bears witness to the terrible things that human beings can do to one another.

Yet her story is also one of survival. Not only did she survive the war, she survived the torturous escape from her homeland as one of the "boat people" of the 1970s. Her story does not end as refugee but it is one of victory and finding a new country to call her own.

I was intrigued and amazed at my friend's determination and courage in face of fear, devastation, isolation, and hopelessness. She has taught me that the problems I face in day to day life can be overcome with faith and fortitude.

This book would not have been possible without the encouragement of two very important people, my husband, Chris Dobbe, and my very dear friend, Peggy Evans. They were terrific cheerleaders and proof readers. I am not sure this book would have been completed without their support. I love you and thank you both for loving me back. Also, Thomas Hodges, who edited this book, has made me sound far more articulate than I really am. I am thankful he took on this project and believed the story was worth telling. And of course, all of Christy's friends and family, primarily her children—Carolyn, Travis, and Steven—who have patiently waited for the end product—thank you for standing by us as we labored with love over this project.

This is Christy's story, as she told it to me over the course of three years—as she has lived it over the course of 53 years.

Patti Dobbe

1

War is unimaginable until you have lived through it. That is *if* you live through it. Then you cannot forget it, no matter how hard you try. War was my life as a child. It has followed me halfway around the world and across the many decades of my life. Even today, my heart beats faster when I hear sounds that resemble helicopter blades beating the air or the noise of footfalls on the forest undergrowth. My story is one of a child who grew up with the sounds of gunfire and bombings as her lullaby. My story is one of an adult still living under the umbrella of prejudice just because I am South Vietnamese. Most of all, my story is one of courage, success, and redemption.

I was born in 1957, the Year of the Rooster, in Bac Liêu, a coastal city in South Vietnam. When I was a child, South Vietnam was an independent state, separate from North Vietnam. We had our own capitol city, Saigon, while Hanoi was the capitol of North Vietnam. *Viet* refers to the type of people who live there, the ethnic groups, while *Nam* means "south." So Vietnam literally means "southern land of the Viet people." South Vietnamese people were different than those who lived in the northern part of the country. There was prejudice and discrimination between the two factions.

Two issues primarily perpetuated the mutual dislike between North and South people. First, the language is different from one another. The South Vietnamese pronounce words differently than North Vietnamese people, and words have varied meanings depending if a North or South person is speaking. Secondly, each of us has a negative view of one another. The North people see us Southerners as being lazy and simple, while we view ourselves as friendly, honest and easygoing. We think of Northerners as cold, cunning, and overly ambitious. There is a mindset of "us" and "them."

Bac Liêu was filled with more than a hundred thousand people. Its streets were congested with motorcycles, bicycles and pedestrians. The open-air markets were filled with the smells of fresh vegetables and seafood cooking. People chatted and bartered back and forth. It was full of life when I was a little girl.

Bac Liêu had several temples. We worshipped Buddha and burned incense to him in our temples. The temple was used as a meeting place by the town council and other important citizens, as well as a place where we celebrated festivals. Temples were colorful with red roofs covering yellow buildings. There was a dragon design both inside and outside of the temple that was brightly painted in greens and yellows. A statue of Buddha was prominently displayed.

Bac Liêu was a wealthy city when I was young because of the seafood industry, the flourishing rice crops, and salt farms surrounding it. Bac Liêu's population was primarily comprised of Vietnamese and Chinese people, with the vast majority, almost 80 percent, being Chinese. I grew up speaking Chinese and Vietnamese since my mother is Chinese. I suppose to be more accurate, I should say that I spoke only one out of more than 100 Chinese dialects.

Vietnam is a product of many cultures. We had been ruled by the Chinese for a very long time. They gave us their religion, writings, and medical practices. Perhaps the most important Chinese influence was Buddhism. Buddhists believe that a person lives many lives and die many deaths, with the ultimate goal of reaching nirvana, which is ultimate peace. Once nirvana is attained, the living and dying cycle ends.

France took Vietnam from the Chinese during the 1800s. Many of the buildings in Vietnam have French architecture. The French also brought Catholicism to Vietnam. Many people chose to become Catholics even though they knew the Vietnamese government could, and often did, punish them for their conversion. I remained a Buddhist up until the time I left the country. Despite French rule and influence, many Chinese people continued to live in Vietnam.

Bac Liêu is a province as well as a city. The province is mostly a river delta area, lying on the coast of the South China Sea. The Mekong River is one of the twelve great rivers of the world and is nearly 2,700 miles long. Bac Liêu is right in the middle of the Mekong Delta. The Mekong River begins in nearby Cambodia and breaks into hundreds of smaller rivers, canals and irrigation ditches that flowed through the area I lived in. These bodies of water eventually empty into the South China Sea. We called the Mekong River *Song Cuu Long*, which means Nine Dragons' River because of all the smaller rivers that flow out of it. Rice paddies prospered in my hometown. Fishing was, and still is, a big source of income. The sea tide rises and pushes all kinds of seafood into the rivers for easy catching. Eventually, the water rushes back out to sea, picks up more seafood, pushes back inland and the cycle continues, especially during the rainy season. Additionally, salt farms flourish and encompass hundreds of acres near Bac Liêu.

The seasons are two extremes, monsoon or drought. It is always warm, with the hottest temperatures being in the mid-90s during March, April and May. From April through October monsoons, called *gio mua*, bring torrential rains. The dirt streets of Bac Liêu become rivers of mud; no one can stay clean. Some storms bring winds and waves that often causes damage to the town. When the sun finally reappears, it becomes a steam bath. The humidity is oppressive, but as a child I really did not notice it as much as I do now when I return to visit. We had no such thing as air conditioning even though some people do now.

The South China Sea was a thirty-minute walk from my home. For about a hundred yards before I got to the water, the mud became so deep it reached my thighs. Walking through it was difficult for a small girl. However, immediately before reaching the water, the mud became a hard, compact sand bar which made running into the ocean possible. The water level only comes up knee high for a long distance into the sea. People walk into the water fully dressed just to cool off their feet and legs.

My Vietnamese birth name was Pham Phuong Anh. I was called Anh, which is pronounced like the American name Ann. I was happy living with my parents, Vui Pham and Bac Tran, my twin sister Tám Út, and our three older sisters, Lai, Lô and Bây. There were numerous extended family members who lived nearby our home. My three older brothers, Đuống, Quang and Tinh, and another sister, Kiên, had left the family home by the time of my earliest memories. Tám Út and I, being twins, were inseparable. We went everywhere together, even venturing into the jungle from time to time. We especially loved to play in the ocean, splashing each other, catching clams, dreaming the day away.

Our nephew, Phi, who was two years older, never paid much attention to us. His father was our older brother Đuống. Phi was often busy helping our father, Vui, and did not have time for silly little girls. Our niece, Thùy, Phi's sister, who was a year younger than us, was a pest, always following us around, wanting to do everything we did. We tolerated her, feeling so much older and wiser. Phi and Thùy had lived with us for about a year, arriving when I was three years old. Their parents had left Bac Liêu to work in another province. Phi and Thùy had initially gone with them, but when I was two years old, Father had had a dream in which he was shown the children were in danger due to the war that had been going on ever since I could remember. So he went to wherever they had been living and brought them back to Bac Liêu. Their parents had not yet returned, so we were stuck with them.

My early years were a carefree time. My parents loved me and life was good. Mother took care of us; she cooked, cleaned our house, and was available to answer our childish questions. She did all these things in spite of not being a well woman. She often seemed to have something wrong with her, either a headache, a backache, or a vague ache elsewhere. Father had to pay a lot of money for her medicine and doctor bills. Even so, she still did her best to take care of us. Years earlier, while living in another area of Vietnam, my parents' first seven children had all died from a mysterious illness, which everyone suspected to be caused by poison that had been sprayed on the rice crops. I was told the children had died within a short time of each other and none had been sick before their sudden illness and death. After their last child died, Father and Mother moved to Bac

Liêu, away from the poisoned rice and sad memories. It was in Bac Liêu they started their second family, beginning with my brother Đuống. I remember Mother often cried.

Mother had a small sugarcane business. Sugarcane was a big crop in South Vietnam because the wet weather was perfect for growing it. She would cut the cane with a long, very sharp knife and then sell it. People drank the cane juice as a treat, much like soft drinks in America. One day, while she was busy cutting the cane, I stood nearby watching her. I decided to reach in for a quick snack when, whack! Mother brought the knife down on the cane and caught my hand too. Fortunately, the wound healed without developing an infection. I learned my lesson the hard way about playing around knives and busy people.

Father worked hard to give us what we needed. He was a rice and salt farmer, which made him rich. He was able to afford Mother's medical expenses and owned lots of jewelry and a herd of water buffalo. In addition to being the owner of numerous rice fields, Father and several other families also gathered salt from the ocean to sell. He was known locally as the "salt manager."

Our home was large by Bac Liêu standards because it had five bedrooms. No one had indoor plumbing for their toilet. Father had built the family toilet on the river behind our house so the current would take our waste out to sea twice a day. We were lucky compared to others who lived in town. Most people had to use public toilets that had privacy doors that came up to their shoulders so as others walked past them, their heads were visible to everyone. The body wastes then collected into ditches dug at the toilet areas, and the smell was awful when you walked by on your way into town. To compound the indignity of doing one's private business where everyone could see, people could only buy a small ration of toilet paper to use each time. The paper was of poor quality, and the amount was hardly enough to do the job properly.

My father was a quiet man who took the time to teach me to swim and laugh. Father was an enthusiastic Buddhist. We had a picture of Buddha hanging on a wall in the house surrounded by several cups of sand that held sticks of incense. Father would light the incense daily and pray to Buddha. Sometimes I prayed to Buddha as well. The whole family would go to the temple on special occasions when several families would meet together to eat, much like church picnics in America.

Near our home was the Giong me River, where I swam every day from ages six to eight. *Giong* means small river. *Me* is known as "tamarind." It is a sticky brown pulp from the pod of a tree of the pea family, widely used in Asian cooking. We commonly used *me* to add flavor to soup.

Giong me was a saltwater river so dirty that the water was brown, resembling Worcestershire sauce! It was composed mostly of sediment and silt the sea swept in during the tides plus all the human waste from the town's population. But I did not care what the water held, for I would swim in it, naked and free. I swam alone most of the time, diving to the bottom and resurfacing with a face that had turned as brown as the water. People who lived nearby would see me in the river, day after day. Some of the older people thought I was an alligator since they could not imagine a human being would play in such a filthy river. But, I felt supremely liberated in that river, my river, floating on top of the saltwater, safe from drowning.

People in their boats would drift nearby me on their way to the market to sell fruits and vegetables. It was common for them to sort through the fruit during their boat trip and toss damaged pieces overboard into the river. I would retrieve the discarded fruit from the brown water and eat it. Sometimes people who lived on one side of the river would ask me to swim to the other side and buy them noodles to eat at the market. I would swim on my back carrying the goods like an otter, holding them on my chest. Life could not get any better than this, I often thought. Every week or so, Mother had to clean the brown grime of the river off me by using lamp oil. She had to scrub my delicate skin raw to get me clean again.

During the summer when I was around four, on a really hot and humid day, my older brother and sister returned home from Ca Mau, a town that was about a four hour drive from Bac Liêu. Ca Mau was at the southernmost tip of Vietnam, and was known to be a very dangerous place. The fighting with the Communists had been intense in that area and, many people had died or fled their homes, with no other option available other than to live in the jungle.

I was outside gathering wood for Mother when Kiên, my sister, and Đuống, my brother, arrived. I did not really know these distant siblings. Both of them seemed too old to be my brother and a sister. They had to be close to thirty years old or so. I had no memory of them even though I had known of their existence. I was only one or two years old when they had left Bac Liêu to work in Ca Mau, where they cut wood to help support the family. I was told they lived on a boat on a river near the jungle. Their life sounded exotic, but now, seeing them for the first time, I was a little intimidated. Kiên was nice and Đuống talked a lot. You have to understand the nature of Vietnamese people. We are not openly loving and demonstrative with one another. We are more reserved, which many people take as being cold and disconnected. But we are not like that. We love each other as much as any other culture loves their family.

The night they came home, Mother prepared a special meal for all of us. Food was plentiful and included soup, a variety of vegetables, steamed rice, pork and shrimp served with *nuoc mam*, a special sauce made out of fermented fish. We all ate so much we thought our stomachs would burst. But we found enough room to stuff down dessert, a wonderful dish consisting of a fried noodle that was covered in coconut milk and sugar. A special treat for sure. The family was very happy to be reunited and have an evening of celebration.

Đuống was a pleasant looking person who loved to hear himself talk. He had all the answers to all the questions, or at least *he* thought he did. However, when things were not done to his liking, he became contentious and loud. He was unpredictable and that scared me. I stayed far away from him. However, Kiên was different from our brother. She was very quiet, like a small mouse, yet friendly. Kiên was a petite woman whose only mission it seemed was to help family members. She did whatever Mother told her to do without complaint. No one ever spoke about their time in Ca Mau. As time went on, I noticed that Đuống liked to drink wine in the afternoons with his friends. He often sent Kiên to the market to keep him supplied with his favorite drink. It was not unusual to see Đuống playing cards, often losing money our family needed to buy food and other supplies. Frequently South Vietnamese soldiers stopped by the house, and my parents would give them food and liquor. We were always trying to appease the soldiers it seemed. Đuống frequently ate with the soldiers and played lively card games after consuming a quantity of liquor.

A couple of years later when I was six, Đuống and Kiên had a surprise for the family. One night after dinner as the family was preparing for bed, Đuống cleared his throat loudly, as if he had something very important to say. We all looked up at him expectantly, waiting to hear his announcement. "Father, Mother, as you know Kiên and I have depended on you to support us and our children these past two years. Well, it is now time for us to make our own place. We will make our home near the river, in the jungle, and start a fishing business. We will take Phi and Thùy, our son and daughter, with us and leave tomorrow."

I was astounded. Đuống and Kiên were married? That could not be, they were brother and sister, my brother and sister! I was so confused. Tám Út and I stole glances at each other. She seemed as off balance as I was. If they were not each other's brother and sister, then who were they to me? It would be some time later before I discovered the truth about these two people.

Father sat there without speaking for several minutes. Mother had begun crying silently, while Kiên, as usual, did not say anything. Finally, Father nodded his head in agreement and said it was time that Đuống took care of his own family. The next day the four of them left, leaving us feeling desolate. Tám Út and I tried to keep ourselves busy throughout the day but discovered we were unsuccessful keeping Phi and Thùy out of our thoughts. We missed that pesky little girl! The house was very quiet that first night. However, we moved on as a family, seeing Đuống and Kiên on rare occasions whenever they came into town for provisions.

In 1965, when I was eight years old, Father brought all of us together and told us about the soldiers. "Do not go anywhere alone," he warned us girls. "The soldiers cannot be trusted to treat you honorably. They are always looking for Viet Cong, who are Communist soldiers from North Vietnam. The South Vietnamese soldiers will hurt anyone they need to if they think you have information about where a Communist lives. Just stay alert and be careful and never find yourself in town without your mother or me with you." Father's face was very serious and stern looking, which was so unlike him.

My country had been at war since before I was born. However, we had not been touched by it as much as the northern and middle parts of Vietnam. But war was always nearby. Tám Út and I looked at each other with concern, wondering what this was all about. We were just little girls. No one could possibly think we were hiding Communists, could they? We did not even know for sure what a Communist was. All we knew about them were the drawings we saw in our school books. They were ferocious looking creatures with long teeth, elongated heads, bulging eyes, and pointy hats. We already knew to stay far away from them.

We were also very familiar with the South soldiers. They had been around all of my life. We had overheard the grownups talking about them and how they would arrest people for no reason and make their families pay money to get them out of jail. The soldiers belonged to the Army of the Republic of Vietnam, sometimes shortened to ARVN, or as it is said in Vietnamese, "ngūoi lính," while the Communists, or Viet Cong, came from North Vietnam and were officially called the North Vietnamese Army—NVA for short. The ngūoi lính were supposed to be on our side, but they were not. The only side they were on was their own. The soldiers did not have any conscience about taking whatever they wanted. It was wise to be fearful of them. It was these South soldiers whom the Americans came to help.

Three years before I was born, the northern half of Vietnam had been ruled by the communist leader Ho Chi Minh. The southern half of the country, which was not communist, was led by Ngo Dinh Diem. When the two leaders could not agree on how to reunify Vietnam into one country, the communists formed the underground organization call the Viet Cong or VC. The VC began killing government officials and in 1958 their attacks escalated. The fighting units used guerrilla warfare. The VC soldiers wore black pajamas which was the standard dress of the South Vietnamese people, thus allowing them to openly move around without being easily identified. It was difficult to know who the good guys were and who the bad guys were. It seemed that Father knew the war had escalated and was drawing closer to Bac Liêu. There were now tens of thousands of VC guerrillas making their way into the Mekong Delta area. But the war still seemed far away for us girls in 1965.

Nonetheless, Tám Út and I listened to Father's warnings and promised to do as he asked. We were obedient children. Vietnamese children are raised to obey their parents without question or argument. We knew the North people, the Communists, would try to take us over if we let down our guard. We knew they were sneaky and hid amongst us, infiltrating our towns and our government. We always had to be vigilant. Not withstanding war knocking on our door, Tám Út and I continued on with our lives as most eight-year olds do, oblivious to the larger world.

Every evening I helped cook dinner for the family. Afterwards, it was my job to wash the dishes, replenish the oil in the lights and feed the chickens, geese and pigs. Once the chores were done, Tám Út and I would go down the street to a neighbor's house to watch television. Even though we had money, Father had not yet bought us a TV set. So, about twenty of us neighborhood children would rush through our nightly duties and run to watch Chinese soap operas. We would eagerly sit outside of the house near the front door and watch the show. Once it was over, we walked back home, excitedly discussing the show's plot or coming up with an ending we liked better than the one we saw.

A few weeks later, one night after we had gone to bed, Tám Út got up when she heard low voices murmuring outside. It was late and the night was very dark. The air was heavy, as it always was in the humid summer heat.

I had remained asleep and was dreaming about swimming in the cool ocean, with large schools of colorful fish swimming by my side, as if I was their leader, the ocean princess. Suddenly, a huge tuna began poking me with his nose, over and over, and then I was rudely aroused from my dream by frantic shaking. It was only Tám Út, not a tuna. "Wake up, Anh, wake up," she whispered in an excited voice. "You must wake up to hear the news I have." "Why don't you leave me alone? I am sleeping and you are bothering me. If you do not quit, I am going to tell Mother," I groggily grumbled at her.

"Listen to me," she said. "You will not believe what I just heard. You are not my sister!" Now she had my full attention. I sat up in bed. What did she mean I was not her sister? I thought I needed to get Mother and have her check Tám Út for a fever. Something was wrong. I had never seen her so agitated. "Stop it Tám Út, you are scaring me. Of course we are sisters, twins, in case you have forgotten. Quick, tell me, what is going on." Tám Út then told me the story that she had overheard.

Tám Út told me how she had been awakened by the sound of agitated voices. Being a curious creature, she had gotten out of bed to see who was speaking and what topic was the cause of so much emotion. Tám Út crept next to the small window in the main area of the house and peeked out. She saw our parents, along with Đuống and Kiên, sitting outside in the moonlight, not too far from the house. Đuống and Kiên had not been to our house in several months, so their presence in the middle of the night was particularly unusual. The four adults spoke in quiet voices but their tone was serious. There was no mistaking that the conversation was important one.

"We often hid in the jungle outside of Ca Mau," Đuống was saying: "the town was too dangerous for us once we left our boat, so we were forced to hide in the dense undergrowth, sometimes for days. The South soldiers, the ngüoi lính, were convinced we were helping the Communists. It did not seem to matter to them that we were always working at honest jobs cutting wood. They followed us and, when they wanted to, the soldiers arrested us, threw us in jail and demanded we tell them all we knew. We did not know anything! They never believed us, but eventually, after days of harassment, they would let us go back to our boat, but continued to follow us around. One day, after getting supplies in town, we returned to the boat and saw the soldiers on board, going through our belongings. They had their guns slung over their shoulders and a couple of them were standing on the dock as look-outs, watching for our arrival. We decided it was not safe, so we hid in the jungle for several days. It was miserable since it was the rainy season, and we could never get dry. Finally, some friends got word to us that it was safe to return to the boat. The soldiers had been sent off to some other province where there was supposed to be a Viet Cong hideout."

Đuống took a deep breath and continued, "That type of torment continued over the next two years. We were always bothered and harassed by the soldiers when we were in town or else we were having to flee and hide out in the jungle. We had to be vigilant at all times and it was so tiresome." Tám Út noticed that Kiên never spoke. She kept her head bowed and it appeared the weight of the world was on her shoulders. "Anyway, that is why we returned home to Bac Liêu. We thought it would be safer if we were all together. Then we get home to find you have sold our home and made our children forget us!" Đuống's voice had taken on an angry tone now.

Father looked at him and said sharply, "Do not speak to me that way, I am your father. I cared for your children these past two years without complaint. I sold your home because it was empty and only field mice were staying there. We needed the money for food, and I did not know if or when you would return. I had not heard from you in more than a year before I decided I had to sell the house. Anyway, if I had not sold it, the soldiers would have just taken it from us, and no one would have received any money at all. So, do not talk to me like I did you a disservice. You, Kiên, and your children now have your new home, and all is as it should be."

Đuống remained silent during his father's berating. He knew he had crossed a line and that the old man had done what was needed during these difficult times. Đuống exchanged a look with Kiên, and then nodded, indicating acceptance of his father's words. Kiên finally spoke up and said, "Thank you for providing a safe home for my children. I cannot ever repay you for your kindness. They seemed healthy and happy while here with you." Her mother-in-law smiled and bowed her head toward Kiên, a moment of tenderness passing between the two women. "However, now we wish to take Anh with us to our new home," Kiên continued, "she should be with us, and with her brother and sister. We need to be a united family."

Father and Mother looked at each other in despair. "But can't Anh stay here? She and Tám Út are so close, they think they are twin sisters. And her schooling is important. She is very smart, one of the best students in the school. It will be devastating for Anh to learn the truth of who you are to her. She thinks we are her parents. What if she hates us for lying to her for all these years?" Mother put her face in her hands, sobbing.

"All right, we will not say anything to her now. But there will come a day, and it will be soon I think, that she will have to come with us. I need her to help with the fishing operation I have set up. Phi and Thùy are not strong enough to do what is necessary by themselves. I am spending too much time helping them when I should be doing other things," Đuống replied. No one said anything else.

Tám Út finished telling me this story and all I could do was stare at her. Father and Mother were not my parents, but rather Đuống and Kiên were? Impossible, simply impossible. And Tám Út, if she was not my twin, then who was she? My cousin? My niece? My aunt? A stranger? I had been lied to by everybody I had loved and trusted since I was born. Tám Út, realizing I was distressed beyond measure, tightly clasped her small arms around me. We held onto each other, wondering why this night had brought us so much sadness. Tám Út then quietly spoke, "We cannot say anything about this. We cannot let them know we know. Maybe you will be able to remain here forever and we can pretend this never happened." But we both knew in our hearts that things had changed and would never be the same.

The next few days were strange for me. I suddenly was not sure what to say to my parents, well, I mean my grandparents. They seemed to be awkward around me too. It felt as if someone had died but no one wanted to talk about it. We kept trying to determine

13

what, if anything, the other knew. It simply grew to be too much to bear.

Finally, a few weeks later, Đuống and Kiên returned to Bac Liêu and had lunch with us. I asked about Phi and Thùy and was told they were unable to come to town because they had to watch over the house. Before they left, Kiên asked me to walk with her to the food market to gather supplies. I felt sick to my stomach, afraid she would talk to me about our relationship and then I could no longer pretend that I was her sister or sister-in-law or whatever we were to one another. As we walked through town, we passed by homes where people were working in their gardens while small children watched them; saw dogs wandering around the streets as if they were on patrol; and, noticed a few soldiers strolling by in a cocky fashion as if they knew no one would challenge them. Thank goodness it was not the rainy season otherwise the dirt streets would have been so muddy that I would have been at risk getting stuck. As we got closer to the market, the smell of fish, fruits and vegetables, goats, pigs and chickens made its way to our noses. I heard the boisterous sounds of people bargaining with each other over prices and quality. I found the sights, smells and sounds comforting. This was my home, where I was at ease.

Kiên did not speak to me until after we had purchased what she needed. We bundled the items neatly together, sharing the load between us. As we headed back home, Kiên started talking about how much she had missed her children while living in Ca Mau and how happy her life would be if all her children were together again. I remained silent, sensing where this was going. As I feared, the conversation turned to me.

"Anh, I do not know how to say this without hurting your feelings, so I will just say it, you are my daughter. I am your mother, not your sister. Đuống is your father, not your brother. I did not say this sooner because I know how close you are to Tám Út, but you need to know the truth. Tám Út is your aunt, Đuống's youngest sister. Her parents are not your parents, but rather, they are your grandparents. You and Tám Út are not twins, but were born just a few months apart. Your grandmother and I were pregnant at the same time with the two of you. Your father and I had to leave Bac Liêu suddenly when you were very small, right after your little sister, Thùy, was born. When we came back a few years later, we realized how much you had grown to love the only family you knew. Thùy was still young enough to grow to love me as her mother and Phi, well, he is a boy who does not want to show his feelings for either me or your grandmother. He only wants his father to be proud of him. So we decided for a little while longer to let you remain with your grandparents and Tám Út, allowing you to believe we were just an older brother and sister who remained distant from you." Kiên paused, as if she needed to gather her thoughts and steady her nerves.

"Why now, why tell me now?" I blurted out before I could stop myself. "Why don't you leave me alone, let me continue with my happy life with my family? Why ruin everything for me?" I started to cry and found I could not stop. Kiên bent down and wiped my tears with her hand. "I know this is difficult for you, but you are a child and can not understand all the reasons. But it is best for you to know the truth. You are old enough now to be told." "Old enough," I thought, "what does she mean 'old enough?' I am only eight years old." But I withheld my thoughts and did not speak them out loud. I knew it would only make things worse.

Kiên said, "You will continue to remain with your grandparents for a while longer, but one day I hope you will want to join the rest of us, your real family, in the jungle. Think about it and we will talk again soon." She stood up and continued walking toward home. Her back was straight as a steel rod. Just like that, the most important conversation of my life was over. I had a million questions but could not get any of them out. We continued home in silence. Once there, I ran to my room and, when I came out hours later, Kiên was gone.

My grandparents knew that I now knew the family secret. That night I sat reading my school book, sulking. I could not concentrate, yet I did not want anyone to talk to me, so I pretended to be engrossed in my reading. However, my father, I mean *my grandfather*, would not let me carry my burden all alone. He sat next

15

to me, put his arm around me and I immediately burst into tears. He patted my shoulder, speaking soothing words and I felt better. Maybe it all would be fine and Kiên would never come back here to mess up my life again. I would just continue on, playing with Tám Út, going to school, doing my chores, and all would be well.

To my dismay, Kiên and Đuống came back to town a month or so later. I knew everyone was watching to see how I would react and if I would treat them respectfully. I felt embarrassed in front of the others, especially Tám Út, but I forced myself to call them Mother and Father, all the while feeling uncomfortable in their presence. After a few visits over the next couple of months, the tensions eased and I began to feel more comfortable around them. After one visit Kiên invited me to return with her to the family home in the jungle to stay for a few days. I thought to myself, "Why not go? I miss Thùy and Phi, and I would like to compare how good my life is to their lives." I agreed to accompany her for a week's visit. I knew I had to return within that time because school was going to start. I liked school and did not want to miss any of it. How was I to know I would never step foot into my school again.

2

Bac Liêu is surrounded by the jungle, thick with ferns, tall grasses, and mangrove trees covered in vines. When I was a child, the jungle was so dense that it was difficult to see other people through the foliage. During the rainy season, the ground turned into a muddy bog. There were holes throughout the jungle filled with standing water. The Viet Cong were known to hide inside the deep, dark tangle of trees and vines. It was common for soldiers from both sides to shoot blindly through the undergrowth to see if anybody was hiding. After a fire fight it was no surprise to walk upon a dead body lying in the shadows of the jungle. By the next day, the body would have disappeared because the soldiers would creep back at night to retrieve their comrade.

The next morning after I had agreed to go with her, Kiên and I woke up early to leave for the family's jungle home. I was scared to be leaving Bac Liêu but excited to venture into the deeper portion of the forest that I had never seen. Kiên took me to the river where she had a small boat tied up. "We have to follow the river. Going by boat is the fastest way," she explained. I climbed aboard, sitting near the back, letting her do all the work paddling us toward our destination. As we left the city behind us, the jungle quickly encroached over the water. Tree branches provided shade for us but also swatted our faces if we did not stay alert and duck in time to avoid the limbs. We were quiet for the first hour. I was entranced with the denseness of the jungle, my eyes straining to see a few feet past the trees and undergrowth. Birds singing, frogs croaking, crabs splashing as they fell off the trees they had climbed, and leaves rustling on the shore from unseen sources excited me. I was so used to the hustle and bustle of a town, that these low undercurrents carried an air of mystery. This was the first time I had gone this far into the jungle. I decided not to worry too much because Kiên seemed unaffected by the noises. If she was not scared, then I was determined not to be either.

After some time had passed by, Kiên started to tell me about her family. "I was raised in a town called Gia Gai. It is about three hours away from Bac Liêu. I am the oldest of eight children. I have two brothers and five sisters. As the oldest, I was expected to take care of all the other children. One of my brothers was killed in the war when he was twenty-three. He was in his camp with his troop when a Viet Cong soldier fired a shoulder rocket into the camp, killing him. Maybe one day you can meet your aunts, uncles, and grandparents."

It is tradition for a Vietnamese woman to leave her family and take her husband's family as her own. The couple usually live with the husband's parents, caring for them in their old age, while the woman's parents are cared for by their sons and daughters-in-law. I remember my mother visited her parents once a year, and I saw them only three times in my life.

Two hours and eight kilometers later, Kiên steered the boat on shore. "We are here," she announced; "the house is just beyond those trees." She pointed to the right but I could not really tell which trees were "those" trees. I just nodded and followed, staying close by her side.

We walked about twenty yards into the jungle when suddenly a small house appeared. The roof was covered with huge leaves that blended with the trees. My brother and sister, Phi and Thùy, came out of the house to greet us. It was awkward at first. I knew I was only a visitor in their world. I could not tell if they resented me for living a life they wish they had or if they felt superior to me because of their way of life. They seemed more grown up than the last time I saw them. We went inside, and I got my first look at my parents' home.

The house was one large room, and the floor was hard-packed dirt. The only furniture was a simple table with five chairs, and two beds. There was a cooking area off to one side of the room. Everyone slept next to each other. The river water stopped only a few feet from the front door, but the house was built up off the ground so the room remained dry during the rainy season. We were isolated out here, I realized. I later learned that this house was where Father and Mother primarily stayed while Phi and Thùy stayed at a different house.

The next day, my brother and sister took me with them to check on the fishing operation, a series of gates along an eleven-kilometer stretch of river. My father owned the land along the river, including another nine kilometers down river. The three houses my father owned were staggered every few kilometers nearby the river. My parents' house was the farthest in the jungle, the one I had stayed at the night before. Down river was another house that was usually unoccupied, except for an occasional visitor the family would hide from the soldiers. I was told the purpose of this empty house was to scare off other people who thought the land and the seafood found in that part of the river was for the taking.

The third house was Phi's and Thùy's home and was closest to the ocean, toward the end of the river. Sometimes, an old man stayed at this house when they were gone, and protected it from nosey strangers. This last house was twenty kilometers, approximately ten miles, from Bac Liêu. The house was built on stilts to protect it from the ocean tide, particularly during the rainy season. Like my parents' home, it too had a dirt floor. As with the other two houses, this one was surrounded by the jungle with the exception of the side that faced the ocean.

It was Phi's and Thùy's responsibility to open the gate at this end to allow the ocean water to flow into the river, bringing with it a multitude of fish and shrimp. The seafood would be swept up the river toward our parents' home where they would open a second gate, trapping the fish and shrimp in a pool located in that upper part of the river. They also had the daily job of chasing off birds that would eat the seafood as it traveled upstream.

I quickly realized how much work it was to chase birds all day long. They never seemed to tire like we did. And, the bird chatter was incessant! I first thought all that noise would make me crazy, but eventually I became used to it. At night, the three of us were alone in the house nearest the ocean. The home had no front door and all manner of creatures crawled and flew inside, such as snakes, moths, birds, and insects. At times, we could hear gunfire back in the jungle. When that happened we would turn off the lights and be very still. We were only seven, eight, and ten years old, living alone in an uncertain world, rife with war.

After about a week with my family, I decided it was time to return to Bac Liêu to be with my grandparents. School would be starting very soon, and since I was the smartest girl in the school, my presence was necessary. One night, my parents had joined us in the ocean-side house for dinner, and I broached the topic of returning to town the next day. "Mother, will we take the boat back up river?" I asked. Father did not even look up when he answered for her, "You will stay here with your true family. You are big enough to work and help your brother and sister with the fishing. In the summer, you will return to your grandparents' home when the drought keeps the fish away. Until then, you will remain here." I sat there stunned. Not go back? Was he crazy? I was only visiting this place; my home was back in Bac Liêu with Tám Út and my other family. I did not know the first thing about living in the jungle, especially alone with two other children while the closest adults were five miles away most of the time. Did they not know it was not safe out here? There was a war going on in this country. The Communists were hiding everywhere, while the South Vietnamese soldiers were being aided by the Americans. Each day it seemed the fighting increased. I had to leave. If my parents wanted to stay, well, that was their business, but I did not want to have anything to do with this type of life.

I looked around at my mother, then at Phi and Thùy, but they all refused to make eye contact with me. My heart sank and tears welled up in my eyes, spilling over before I could stop them. "No," I said, "I must leave tomorrow. Grandfather is expecting me." Đuống stopped eating and gave me a look that sent chills up my spine. "I will send word to him that you will not be coming back. Now eat;

we must go check the gate and nets before sunset. There will be no more talk of you leaving." I could not eat another bite.

Over the next few days, I thought up wild plans of escaping this place. Once, I made up my mind that I would just simply walk out of the jungle back to civilization. I knew the boat ride was only two hours long. I could walk the distance in half a day. The day of my escape came at the end of my third week there. At sunrise, we got up and went about completing the assigned chores Father had given us. I watched Phi and Thùy from the corner of my eye, and when they were busy further into the jungle, I took off. "I can do this, "I am eight years old and very smart," I thought to myself. I set off at a run, jumping over ferns and short grass mounds, going around trees, always staying aware of noises to be sure it was not a South soldier or a Communist.

Then I came to a water crossing. It was one of numerous bodies of water that branched off from the Mekong River. Some of these areas were really more like swamps, full of vegetation, tree branches, and soil. I could not see what was in the water. After I had crossed a couple of small rivulets, I felt confident about my adventure. This was going to be easy. I came upon a larger pool that was more than chest-high. I began pushing through the water when I felt something sharp on my foot. I was being bitten! I pushed as fast as I could through the water, breathing heavily and feeling frantic. There was something holding onto my foot that would not let go, and it felt as if my foot was on fire. I finally reached the other side of the river bank and clawed my way out of the water. Clinging to my foot was a crab. I picked up a rock and began beating it as hard as I could, crying the whole time. The crab let go after a few solid whacks with the rock and scuttled back into the water. My foot hurt worse than any other time I could remember. But I breathed a sigh of relief knowing it was a crab and nothing more. A person could not die from a crab bite, could they? Wait until Tám Út heard about my jungle adventures; she would be so envious of me. I started to laugh with relief, believing I would soon be back in civilization.

I kept on walking, growing thirsty and hungry. "Why had I not thought about bringing any food and water? Oh well, when I get home Grandmother will take care of me," I consoled myself. A little while later, I came upon another water crossing that was about three feet deep, which was pretty deep for an eight year old girl. Now that I was aware of the crabs, I wrapped my feet with leaves to provide a cushion in the event one latched onto me. Feeling clever, I waded in. After a few steps, a movement caught my eye. I stopped dead in my tracks. What was it? I looked around me, standing very still. There, a ripple in the water was quickly moving toward me. It was a snake and it had seen me and was coming closer. I screamed and turned around, back tracking my steps. My legs were pumping as hard and as fast as they could go. The snake was gliding effortlessly toward me. I pushed with all my strength and hurled myself onto dry ground. I looked over my shoulder and watched as the snake slid noiselessly past the spot I had just vacated. At that moment, I realized I could not walk out of this jungle alone. I was destined to remain here with people I did not know, in a life I could not have imagined living only a few weeks ago. I wearily got up and began my journey back into the jungle. I cried the whole way, carrying a broken heart with me.

3

After my disastrous attempt to walk out of the jungle, I pretended a few times to be very sick, so sick that the only reasonable thing for my parents to do would be to take me back to Bac Liêu to see the doctor. Of course, I was living with unreasonable people and my scheme did not work. Mother would feel my forehead, declare me fever-free, and Father would say I would be fine. I quickly realized I was here to stay.

At times, the three of us children would stay in my parents' house whenever they had to go to Bac Liêu to sell the fish and shrimp. Often, it was Phi and Mother who went into town for the day to sell our catch. It was imperative the house always looked occupied so soldiers or other jungle dwellers would not take it over or burn it down. Sometimes, Mother would come to our house near the ocean and stay with us two girls while Phi would stay with Father in the jungle. But, mostly, the three of us were on our own. Every few months, we were allowed to return to our grandparents in Bac Liêu and stay a few nights. It felt good to be back with them, even if it was a short visit. I was so happy those days, being in a real home and not having to work so hard. Then it would all come to a sad end when Father would take us back with him to the jungle. It seemed there was always work to be done.

As time went on, I learned more about my father, what made him happy and what made him mad. He was very nice, until he became upset with us. Father was three years older than Mother and had been married once before. The story was that he was mean to his first wife causing her to run away from him. When Mother met

Father, she was eighteen years old and he was twenty-one. She had had no idea about his temper. Upon marrying Father, Mother left her family and moved to Bac Liêu with Grandfather and Grandmother, until she and Father were able to buy their own home, the home Grandfather later sold while they were in Ca Mau. It is common for Vietnamese mothers-in-law to be unforgiving and difficult women toward their son's wife because the daughter-in-law took their son away. But my mother was fortunate that Grandmother was not like that. Grandmother accepted my mother into the family and treated Mother with dignity. It was Grandmother's son—my father—who treated Mother badly.

Vietnamese husbands have the right to chastise their wives. Mother was a very quiet woman who accepted my father's angry outbursts in order to prevent him from berating us children. Mother would tell us to run and hide from him when he was in one of his black moods. She would cower down before him. Afterwards, when we would quietly return, Phi and I would complete her chores that Father expected to be done by day's end. We knew that she endured unpleasant things that were often meant for one or all of us. Mother left Father once for about a week, but returned to him because she knew without her presence, my siblings and I would be fair game for Father's anger. The day she returned, no words were spoken between them; she just picked up her chores for the day as if she had never left. No one ever mentioned her absence.

Not too long after I realized that living with this family was going to be my destiny, Phi and I were working on the fish nets together. It was a hot and steamy day; the humidity must have been 100 percent. I asked Phi, "Have you ever seen a real Communist? I have read about them in my school books and know only what Grandfather told us about them." He looked up at me, a knowing smile on his face, which was a surprise because he rarely smiled. "Mostly they come out at night so the darkness hides them. But, yes, I have seen a few. I could show you one if you really want," he replied. The thought of seeing a real live Communist was scary yet exciting. "Yes," I said breathlessly, "I want to see one. Not up close where they could catch and kill me, but close enough that I can really see if their teeth are long and pointy." Phi laughed and agreed to take me soon.

A few days later, Father came to our house and told us which chores he wanted us to complete over the next couple of days. He promised he would be back by the week's end to check to see if the chores were finished. He left the next day, and Phi and I set about building the crates and baskets we used to carry the fish to market. Thùy remained at home cleaning the house and doing other small chores that a six-year old could be trusted with.

After he was sure that Father had left the area, Phi asked me "Are you ready to go see a Communist?" The suggestion was unexpected yet I had been waiting for this moment. "Now?" I asked, "What about Father's instructions to get these chores finished by the time he gets back?" Phi assured me that we had plenty of time to go Communist-hunting and still accomplish Father's orders. "They have a camp not too far from here. It will only take us a few hours. We will be back by lunchtime." "How do you know they will be there and not doing some soldier duties elsewhere?" I asked. "Remember, I told you they only leave the safety of their camp in the cover of darkness. They will be there at this time of day, sleeping and planning their next attack. Now is the best time to see them," he reassured me. Phi was ten years old and he was wise about the ways of the Viet Cong.

We left without telling Thùy where we were going. She did not need to know because she would only tell and get us in trouble anyway. We walked further into the jungle than I had ever been before. After a couple of hours of searching, we heard something behind us. The underbrush was moving and someone was breathing hard. "It is a Communist coming to kill us," I thought in a panic. All of a sudden the loudest scream I had ever heard rose up into the sky.

"It is Father," Phi yelled, "run." Father had spied on us to see if we worked like he had told us to, then followed us into the jungle. When he realized we were on a mission of our own and not tending to his business, he completely lost his temper. He began screaming at us, so much so I could not understand his words. But I clearly understood his tone. "Hide with me," I whispered hoarsely; "he will hit you like he does Mother. Please Phi, stay with me." I began to cry. He did not answer me. I hid under a bush and watched as Phi walked toward Father. Phi knew that eventually he had to face the wrath of this man, having lived with him long enough to know putting off the punishment would only increase its ferocity.

Father told Phi to lie down, which he did, then Father began hitting him with the biggest stick he could put his hands on. Phi just lay there and took the swings and the verbal abuse. I cringed each time I heard the whack of branch meeting skin. After he was finished with Phi, Father began yelling for me to show myself. The longer he yelled the angrier he became. He threatened to kill me if he ever saw me again. I was terrified. I did not come out of hiding all day. By nightfall, I returned to the house and fortunately Father had emotionally exhausted himself and did not even look at me. I narrowly escaped the same severe beating that my poor brother endured. That evening, I felt awful that I had gotten my brother into such trouble. I had no idea the depth of my father's anger and how savage he could be with us. As I had expected, Phi was mad at me, but he saw my tears and knew I was sorry. He eventually forgave me and we did not speak of it anymore.

Life began to be more exciting around 1966 and 1967. The pace of the war with the North Vietnamese escalated. The South Vietnamese soldiers, the ngūoi lính, were always known to be mean, often tricking people into admitting they had helped the Communists, whether they did or did not. These admissions resulted in people being jailed for days, weeks and months, unless their family had money to pay for their release. It was not unusual in Bac Liêu for the soldiers to rape the women, kill whomever they did not like, and then steal the victims' belongings. It was these soldiers that the Americans were helping.

The jungle was a hideout haven for the Communists. The soldiers were from North Vietnam and had infiltrated the mountains and jungles of the country all the way to the southernmost area, which is where we lived. The Communists did not have military uniforms, which made it more difficult to discern who they were when you came upon a person in the jungle. Often the South soldiers, the ngūoi lính, would dress like the Communists, in casual clothing and t-shirts, and pretend to be a Communist just to see if you would help them out with food, shelter or information. We learned at a very early age to respond to most questions asked by any stranger by saying, "I don't know." That phrase was our only way out of a difficult and often dangerous situation when encountering either a Communist or a South soldier. We could not risk that we knew who we were talking to, a Communist or a ngūoi lính. If the soldier was a Communist and wanted something from us, we took the chance of being killed if we refused to help. If the soldier was a South soldier and questioned if we had helped the Communists, we took the chance of being killed or arrested if we gave the wrong answer. Either way, both sides often dealt out death if the soldier did not like our responses. "I do not know" seemed to be the only satisfactory answer.

The ngūoi lính wore green fatigues, a red neck scarf and pointy hats. They tried their best to look like the American soldiers even though they failed at the attempt. We rarely saw American soldiers since most of their fighting took place further north, more up-country from us. But when we did, they always gave candy to us children. We would run after them, crying out for more, and they would throw it to us. We liked the Americans, but did not like them helping the South soldiers. The Americans only knew a Communist when the South soldier pointed one out to them. As a result, sometimes innocent citizens were killed by the Americans who believed they were shooting at Communists, but they had actually been lied to by the South soldiers.

One night in 1966, when I was nine years old, my family was sharing a meal together, which was a rare event since we often stayed at the different houses. As we ate, we heard loud guns go off close by the house. We all scrambled out of the house to hide in the jungle. I ran with Father while my brother and sister ran with Mother in a different direction. I was so scared. I had never heard such big guns, much less so close to my home. We hid deep among the tangle of trees and vines. Mosquitoes buzzed around our faces and bit my arms, but all I could do was endure it. We had no idea what happened to my mother and siblings, if they had been captured or shot, or were safely hidden. My small body started shaking and would not stop. Finally, after several hours of quiet, Father said it was safe to return home. We arrived first, and a short while later, the rest of the family showed up. To our dismay, the dog and cat had eaten our dinner that we had left, so we all went to bed hungry. But sleep was impossible that night for me. I prayed to Buddha to please let me go back to Bac Liêu, but my prayers were not answered for a long time.

Later that year, I was staying at my grandparent's home in Bac Liêu during one of my visits. One morning my older aunt, Aunt Lai, was removing a pan of hot water off the stove in order to make tea for Grandfather. Tám Út and I were running through the house, enjoying some free time together playing instead of working. As I ran by Aunt Lai, I hit the pan of boiling water with my arm and the water poured all over my left side, burning me badly. I began screaming and dancing around wildly, tearing at my clothes. The pain was indescribable. My skin was seared. Grandmother came running into the room and tried to grab me so she could take a look at my injuries. I could not be consoled and did not allow her to touch me. Finally I exhausted myself and slumped to the floor. Grandmother saw how serious the burns were and began putting medicine on them. I was sent to bed, but the touch of any clothes or sheets caused intense pain. I was at Grandmother's home for a month healing from the burns. I still carry the scars from the hot water on my left side, but I was fortunate that Grandmother had the right medicine that prevented infection from setting in. People were known to die from such injuries as mine during that time.

After I had sufficiently recovered from my burns, Phi came to town to check on me and visit our family. A local movie theater was showing a John Wayne movie that was full of cowboys and Indians, so Phi offered to take me. It was the first time I had ever seen a large screen movie. I started to get scared after seeing so many Indians get killed. I believed it was real life and refused to go by myself to the bathroom until the killing stopped. I was afraid that as I sat on the toilet, people would fall on me after getting shot by John Wayne. When I did go, I hurried as fast as I could to get out in case the Indians came back and the shooting started all over again.

The second movie I saw was the animated film *Cinderella*. I was amazed at the story and entranced with Cinderella's beauty. We watched it twice. Phi and I decided we wanted to see it a third time, but wanted to wait and take our sister, Thùy. She loved it as much as we did. This movie was real life as far as I was concerned. I wondered when my fairy godmother would appear.

The Communists loved to show movies in the local theaters telling everyone how they were winning the war. One of their movies highlighted female Viet Cong soldiers. These women were dressed in all black, the traditional pajama-style clothing that the VC were famous for wearing, and had a striped scarf draped across their shoulders. They were in a canoe that contained a load of dynamite. As night fell, the female soldiers crept into a town to set a bomb made with dynamite as many nguoi lính as possible, along with a tank manned by the South soldiers. As I watched, my eyes glued to the movie screen unable to look away, I began shaking in fear. I knew I had to return to the jungle, where the Viet Cong soldiers also lived, who only wanted to kill South Vietnamese people. I realized even though they preferred to kill soldiers, I knew they would kill whoever was around. I was very afraid for myself and my family. I was nine or ten years old by now, and already knew too much about fear and death.

After the movie ended, Phi and I began walking back to our boat to return to our home in the jungle. We passed by the Bac Liêu police station, and being silly children, both of us ran by the police officers standing outside and yelled, "Hurry, the bomb will blow; get out of the way." We did not understand the ramifications of our joke until one officer stopped us and asked harshly where the bomb was. We told him it was in the movie we had just seen and it was not a real bomb. He reprimanded us and threatened to put us in jail for making such a joke. Both of us began crying and apologized for our stupidity. Thankfully, he let us go on our way, just shaking his head at us. Everyone took war seriously in those days, and if you forgot to, then someone made you remember the horrors it brought.

In 1967, when I was ten years old and had been in the jungle for two years, my father was arrested by the South soldiers and accused of helping the Communists. The soldiers came to our house in the jungle and grabbed Father before he could hide. They demanded to know what help he had provided the Communists who had recently come through the area. He kept saying he did not know or do anything, but they did not believe him. They took him to jail in town and tortured him with electrical shocks. They placed electrodes on his thumbs and big toes. When he did not give them the answer they wanted to hear, they turned the dial higher until he passed out. After a few unsuccessful tries with electricity, the soldiers then dragged him to another area where they hit him and immersed his head in mud and water. "Tell us where the Communists are hiding," they demanded. But, he really did not know. All he knew was that they were somewhere in the jungle, but everyone knew that. Eventually, after Grandfather paid them some money, the soldiers let Father out of jail. He returned to us weakened, yet determined not to tell either side anything. After this experience, Father was quiet and tired more easily than before. At night, we would hear him yell in his sleep, screaming at his nightmares.

These arrests and periodic torture sessions happened two to three times a year to Father. He was usually released after a week, but there was one time he was held for two months. About the time the family had saved some money, we would have to give it to the soldiers for his bail. The amount of money the family had to pay was enough to build a house in those days. Once I went to the jail in Bac Liêu to visit Father and was only able to see him from a distance through the fence. The guards had put Father in charge of cooking for all the prisoners. I watched as he prepared the meal in the big pot and suddenly realized the pot had never been cleaned. It was used from one meal to the next, from one day to the next without ever being washed. The guards did not think the prisoners deserved sanitary conditions. As a result, it was common for the prisoners to become sick with dysentery and other intestinal ailments. Our family was always sad when Father was in jail because we knew he was suffering. Also, it was difficult to keep up with the fishing operation duties without him. Life was tough for all of us in those days.

One afternoon, Father was at our grandparents' house in Bac Liêu. A South Vietnam soldier—a ngūoi lính that Father knew—stopped by and Father invited him to share the meal. Father and this soldier ate and drank together, laughing and talking as men do. After several hours, the soldier finally stood up to leave and said, "Now, you must come with me." Father just looked at him blankly, and asked why. "I must take you to jail as my prisoner. That is why I came here in the first place. No more talk, let's go." Everyone was stunned. This man had been acting as if he were my father's best friend, laughing and drinking Grandfather's liquor. Now he was arresting Father for no apparent reason. Father knew better than to argue the point, so he got up and allowed himself to be taken to jail. After about a week, Mother was able to gather up enough money to post bail and get him out.

Because of these experiences, whenever Mother and Father would hear people coming toward the house or heard other noises that they could not identify, they ran and hid in the jungle, leaving us children alone in the house to deal with whatever appeared. Children could be scared, threatened or taken advantage of, but they were not arrested and tortured. My parents knew this.

Even though the South soldiers had warned us about the evil ways of the Communists, the Viet Cong were nicer to us than the ngūoi lính. The South soldiers never hesitated to walk into our houses, the house in the jungle or the one we children lived in near the ocean, and take whatever they wanted. On many occasions, they had come in through our open door, taken our food, ransacked our belongings, and stole our chickens and other animals. The soldiers had no respect for our home or us. All we could do was just cower in the corner and ask politely for them to leave some food for us. Sometimes they did, but most times they took everything, making us start all over the next day gathering food and buying more animals. After they would leave, we had to work for hours cleaning up after them because they had worn their muddy boots inside the house and tossed around our belongings, looking for money, jewelry, anything they believed was valuable. Of course, they said they were looking for evidence that a Communist had been there. Ha . . . they were just thieves wearing a soldier's uniform. They came around once or twice a month and all we could do was endure the intrusion.

My family never became Communist, but when they won the war, Father was glad that he would not be taken to jail on a moment's notice without any reason like the South soldiers had done to him repeatedly. Little did we know until later that the Communists had other ways of keeping people down, of destroying lives . . . they would one day take most of Father's land without any compensation.

4

One night my brother, sister and I were staying in the house in the jungle, taking care of our parents' home while they had gone to Bac Liêu to sell our latest seafood catch. We had been alone for about a week, doing the chores Father had instructed us to have finished by the time he returned in a couple of weeks. We had learned our lesson to always obey Father after Phi had received the beating when we went on our "Communist hunt." While we were sleeping a distant thumping sound woke us up. It was similar to the noise of a motor off in the distance. We held our breath and listened intently. It grew louder and louder, and we suddenly realized it was a helicopter. We scrambled to extinguish the lights we had left on that provided us a small measure of comfort. We knew the lights would alert the pilot as to the location of our house, and let him know that people were home. As Father had told us, we lay down on the lower portion of the floor that had been dug into the hillside, which provided some protection in case the helicopter shot at us. This night we were fortunate. The pilot did not see us and flew on by. There was no more sleep for us that night.

A few months later, while at grandmother's home, I received a second serious burn. Grandmother had a pot of boiling water on the stove, and somehow I managed to pull it off and onto my leg. The pain was unbelievable. How in the world had I managed to do this again? Instead of calling out for help, feeling somewhat stupid over my clumsiness, I ran out of the house and sat in my beloved Giong me river to cool off my leg. I sat there for hours, until the sun started setting. I then went back home, and Grandmother was upset with me because she had no idea where I had been all that time. I showed her my leg, and she immediately ran to get the medicine. I was again fortunate in that infection did not set in. However, as the skin fell off as it healed, I was left with more scars. It seemed that I was going to be as scarred as an old war soldier but I was turning out to be my own worst enemy.

In 1967 the fighting escalated between the Communists and the South soldiers. It was not unusual to hear the thump of artillery and the spitting sound of automatic weapons, sometimes close to the house. One hot and humid day, Father and I were working around my parents' home, the one in the jungle, while the rest of the family had gone to check the fish nets. We heard distant gunfire that was slowly getting closer to us. As was the usual custom, soldiers were randomly shooting in front of them while walking through the dense vegetation, hoping to kill a hidden enemy or scare out any person who had the bad fortune to be in the forest at that moment. It sounded as if there were at least two hundred of them. Father looked at me and said urgently, "Run, Anh, and hide. Do not let them see you. They will kill you." I heard the fear in his voice. We ran in opposite directions as fast as we could.

I happened to be wearing a brown shirt that day, of all days. You see, the Communists' had very tan skin because they were in the sun most of the time and often did not wear a shirt. I pushed through the jungle, not caring that the tall grass and low hanging branches slashed at my face, arms and legs. "Hurry," I thought, "do not stop; they are close, so close." My breath was coming in gasps, my heart was beating hard enough to make my ears pound. I heard sounds closing in behind me. Sweat poured down my face, stinging my eyes. I knew I must hide quickly before I was spotted by the men who chased me. I dove into a thicket of grass and low bushes lying at the base of a huge tree, and pushed myself as far back into the covering as I could. I placed my hands over my mouth to keep my breathing as quiet as possible. Mosquitoes buzzed in my ears, tickling my face. I had to resist slapping at the pests. Quiet—I knew I had to be ever so quiet and become invisible or die.

I heard the men lunge through the forest sounding like bulls; then all became still. Suddenly, the reeds were yanked back, and the men smiled at me, pointing their guns at my face. I screamed until I lost my breath.

I was face to face with two South soldiers. I imagined I could smell their breath, but, perhaps I only smelled my own fear. The closest man was pointing his gun at me as if he was about to pull the trigger. His face was intense, all taut with adrenaline. My screams did not seem to register in his mind that I was a little girl. The second man saw me for what I was and immediately pushed his partner's gun up in the air. "Do not shoot; she is just a child," the man yelled at him. The gunman visibly exhaled and relaxed his shoulders. "What are you doing out here, you foolish girl?" the man demanded. "Do you not know there is a war out here? You could get shot, and no one would find your body until the animals got through eating you." I just stared at them, unable to speak. I had no idea what to say to a soldier, afraid they would probably kill me regardless how I responded.

They sat down near me for a while, talking to each other in low tones. I had no idea what they were saying. I sat there, shivering, saying my prayers to Buddha. Finally, they said I needed to wait with them while the rest of their troop cleared the area of VC soldiers. So we waited, none of us speaking. After a few hours, the man who saved me from getting shot said I could leave. "But you need to be more careful. This jungle is no place for a child. One day, someone who is not as nice as us will find you and do unspeakable things to you. You better go home and stay there."

I ran away from them as fast as I could go. When I got home, Father was already there. He just looked at me and did not say a word, going about his business as if it was another normal day in the jungle.

The next day, my brother Phi and I were out in our canoe, checking on the fish nets. The day was hot and sultry, the sun shimmering off the water. As the boat glided on the river, the small motor puttering, we saw something up ahead. It looked like a fallen tree or some other debris floating in our path. As we got closer, we realized it was a canoe. We drifted up next to the boat, thinking it was peculiar for a boat to be out here without anyone in it. Canoes were the primary mode of transportation for most of us jungle dwellers; thus they were a precious item, so this was unusual.

As we pulled up alongside the drifting canoe, we saw a woman lying in it. She was dead. We saw she had been shot in both knees. She was laying on her back, her blood was mixed with the water from the river and covered the bottom the canoe. Phi and I realized we knew this woman. She, her husband, and their young son lived nearby our grandparents' home in Bac Liêu. We later learned the woman had been walking alone through the jungle, when soldiers shot her and threw her in the canoe, and pushed it out into the current to float away. She must have bled to death or possibly died of dehydration in the sweltering heat; I never knew for sure. However, it was strange and disquieting to see the dead woman. We stared at her for a minute and then let the water pull us away from her. We were silent for a while, wondering about the insane time in which we were living.

We continued floating down the river, feeling the disquiet slowly leave us as the hours passed. Neither of us felt like talking and I was left to my thoughts of the woman, wondering if her husband was yet looking for her or was at home, waiting for her to return to cook his dinner. The noises of insects and bird calls calmed our jittery nerves.

We began to allow ourselves to enjoy the lazy feel of the day, especially after my experience the day before when I was nearly shot to death. Suddenly I heard Phi inhale sharply, causing me to look up at him. He was staring toward the shoreline. I turned my head in that direction and saw two South soldiers on the river bank. They shot their weapons up in the air. "Oh please, not again," I moaned to myself. They shouted at us to come to them, waving their semiautomatic guns. We did as they instructed, feeling dread in the pit of our stomachs. Yesterday I was shown respect by the soldiers and was not harmed. But the South soldiers had a reputation of taking whatever and whoever they wanted. I trembled at the thought they were going to kill us, feeling certain they were the same soldiers who had killed that poor woman we had seen earlier.

As we pulled closer to the land, Phi whispered to me under his breath, "Do not say anything. Let me talk to them. Just do whatever I do." I was only too happy to comply. He was, after all, twelve years old and knew so much more than I.

As soon as we got near them one of the soldiers jumped into our boat and grabbed my arm. He started pulling me off the boat. I could smell the liquor on him, and knew he was drunk. I struggled against him while Phi started pleading with the man to leave me alone. "Please sir, she is my sister, just ten years old. Let her stay with me. We are tending our father's fishing nets like he asked us, and he is waiting on us to return home. Please sir, let us go. We are no threat to you. We do not have any money or weapons." I pleaded, "Oh Uncle," ("uncle" was a term of respect that young people used when speaking to older men), "please let me go and do not hurt me. My brother and I are not doing anything wrong. We are just obeying our father and doing as he has told us." I was shaking like a leaf in the wind. I had heard enough stories from my parents, grandparents, and friends about the horrible things the soldiers did to young girls. I was terrified of these men, particularly after seeing how the woman in the canoe had been shot and left to die all alone.

The man kept his grip on my arm, looking undecided. The other soldier said, "Let her go. She is too young anyway. I do not want one that young. There are plenty of others for us." The man let me go, giving me a little push and causing me to stumble backwards into the canoe. He sneered at us, turned and walked away. Phi and I looked at each other, and then he slowly pushed the canoe back out into the river channel. We both knew we were lucky that Phi was not shot and thrown into the water and that I was not raped, then killed. We realized that life could end at any moment or at the least, any type of horrible thing could happen. What a heavy burden for a ten-year old girl to carry.

Later that year, 1967, I experienced the terror of napalm, a liquid fire that destroyed everything it touched. I was visiting my grandparents in town when a plane dropped it on the jungle about one and a half miles from their home. Thankfully it did not reach us, but many families were killed or seriously wounded. Townspeople ran into the jungle after the bulk of the fire died down to see if there was anyone that they could rescue. Only one family was brought out and taken to the hospital. The four children, three daughters and a son, were burned severely, so much so that their ears were gone. These children survived and continue to live in Bac Liêu as adults, and all of them look like a caricature of a person. It gives me chills to see how badly their skin was damaged and how pretty children could be so quickly turned into a replica of a movie monster. I become sad whenever I think about their struggles.

The war took a toll on families in ways other than physical injuries. People were under immense stress all the time. Relief and laughter were hard to find. Violence in families became commonplace; wives were beaten by their husbands, and some husbands were struck as well. One day while I was standing at my grandparents' doorway enjoying a view of the lake, I heard loud angry voices. I looked toward the lake and saw a woman and her husband fighting with each other, the man getting the worst of the injuries. Both were drunk. His wife pulled the two of them into the lake, hitting him as hard as she could. Other adults were watching the scene and no one did anything to help either of them. They eventually tired and sloshed their way back to shore.

Another couple who lived near my grandparents became involved in an argument with one another. I saw the wife throw a fistful of dirt on her husband's shirt. This enraged him so much that even I became afraid. I cowered down but could not take my eyes off the scene. The man grabbed his wife and began pulling her toward the lake. She struggled against him but to no avail. He thrust her head into the water and held her there. The woman thrashed around, her hands trying to pull her husband's hands off the back of her head. He only pushed her down harder. I looked around and saw other people congregating in the area, transfixed on the couple but no one moved forward to intervene. After a few minutes, the woman's movements ceased. Her body began floating and her hair fanned out around her head in the water. She had drowned. Her husband released his grip and stood up. He pulled her lifeless body to the shoreline and sat down heavily next to her. I watched a few more minutes but he did not move. I slipped quietly away and the other bystanders returned to their business, all of us leaving the man alone. The next day the woman's body was gone, and no one spoke of the incident.

The parents in a third family who lived in the same neighborhood also fought with each other. The man was a South soldier and had always seemed to be a nice and gentle person to his wife and children. But even nice people were known to break under the stress of continuous warfare. Only a few days after witnessing the husband drown his wife, I heard this couple arguing through the open windows of our two homes. Since I was friends with their children, I felt compelled to run to their house to see what was going on. This couple was not known to be loud with one another, which made the shouting even more disturbing to hear.

As I neared the house, I saw the man hold his wife up against a wall, yelling at her. I stopped running, realizing I did not need to get in the middle of whatever was happening. But I watched, unable to contain my curiosity. The man let go of his wife, placed his left hand on the wall next to her head, and then quick as lightening, he raised a sharp knife he had been holding in his right hand and cut off his own finger. His wife screamed, perhaps fearing her face would be cut next. Blood was on the wall, on the floor and on both of the people. I was shocked. I started to run home. If he did chop up his wife, I did not want to see that happen. As far as I know, the detached finger was the only fatality that day in that family.

5

My father was too old to be a soldier by the time the Communists brought the war to South Vietnam. Before Father moved Mother and us children to the jungle, he and two of his friends had gone into the area to decide if they could make a living there and find a place to build a home. After the three of them had stopped for the night and set up camp, South soldiers came upon them unexpectedly and beat them up. The soldiers checked all three of their identification cards and saw Father's two friends were younger than he. So those men were taken away to become soldiers. Father was left behind since he was considered far too old to be soldier material.

Even though he may have had leanings toward the Communists since they were not as ruthless as the South soldiers, Father was still determined not to become a Communist. I know my father had to pay taxes to both sides, the North and the South, in order to work the land, which required him to portray himself as sympathetic to whomever he was dealing with at any particular moment. It was a difficult game to maintain at all times.

It was not unusual for South soldiers to terrorize families just for fun. Often, upon approaching a house in the jungle, the soldiers were known to kill all the family's animals, leaving the people without food or a source of income. Communist soldiers never did that. Rather, they would ask for food. They treated people with more respect than the South soldiers.

Whenever my family would go to Bac Liêu to sell our fish and shrimp and restock our supplies, South soldiers would follow us around town to see what and how much we purchased. They were interested to find out if we bought more medicine and food than we needed as a family. This was how they would determine if we were helping the Communists. We had to be very careful to watch what we took back to the jungle with us in order to keep the soldiers' suspicions to a minimum. This often limited us as to what we would have to eat.

Even with this intense scrutiny, I know Father helped the Communists from time to time. When I was ten years old, I was standing outside of my house when I saw a man coming toward me. I ran and called for Father to come. The man approached us and asked for food. Then I saw his arm; it was bloody and hanging limply by his side. He had been shot. Father told him to wait in the cover of the trees and turned to go inside the house. He came back outside carrying a bowl of rice. As he walked toward the young man he stopped and turned to speak to me. He told me to never tell anyone about this man coming to our house or that Father had given him food. If I did talk about it I would cause all of us to be killed or imprisoned. I promised I would not. Father then took the rice to the wounded soldier. I do not know whatever happened to that man but Father and I never spoke of the incident again.

A few months later, when Father was gathering wood and the rest of us were busy with our chores, we all heard an airplane flying low, heading in our direction. Suddenly the plane came over the trees, very low and close to us. The ground all around Father began erupting and spraying his legs with dirt. I heard loud cracking and spitting sounds over the airplane's engines. Machineguns on the plane were strafing all around my father. He ran as fast as he could but was struck in the leg. He jumped into the lake for cover, and then the plane flew past us. We all ran to the lake and pulled out Father. He needed to go to the hospital in Bac Liêu, so Mother took him in a small motor boat. He remained in the hospital for about a month with Mother staying with him the entire time. That left us children in the jungle house by ourselves. Periodically a family member would check on us and stay a few nights. But for most of the month, we were on our own. We had to take care of the house, the fishing operation, and each other.

Father eventually recovered sufficiently from his leg wound and returned home. However, until he got his full strength back, Mother was in charge of taking the fish to town to sell. A few weeks after Father's return home, Mother and Phi left for town and would be gone a few days. Thùy and I had the chores to do all by ourselves plus take care of Father. Father was not any help except for giving us orders. By the end of each day, we were exhausted.

The third day after Mother's and Phi's departure, Thùy and I were outside feeding the animals. We had a few chickens, thirty ducks, three cats, seven dogs, and a couple of pigs. One pig was only a few months old and weighed about fifteen pounds. He was unusual because he was completely white, not a hint of pink on him. He was so cute and liked to follow me around. One day he would be big enough to either eat or sell.

On this particular day, Thùy and I heard fighting coming from the jungle and toward the house. We yelled for Father, who was inside, and he limped outside with us. He told me to run, pointing out a pathway, and he took Thùy with him to hide in another direction. They disappeared among the trees. I started running and then I heard a sound at my heels. I whirled around and saw the small white pig chasing after me with all his might. We ran together toward the lake, the sounds of gunfire getting closer. I knew a good place to hide was among the reeds and other vegetation in the water. I jumped in and looked around, seeing the pig follow after me. He stayed right with me, evidently just as scared as I was. We hid for a while until the gunfire subsided. Slowly we made our way out of the water.

As soon as we were on dry land, out of nowhere, came three huge, wild dogs. They barked madly and lunged at me and my pig. I was crying and screaming at them when I saw a big stick lying nearby. I grabbed the stick and began swinging it wildly. About the time I thought my pig would be eaten and I would be mauled to death, a shot rang out. I spun around and there stood an older South soldier, his gun up to his shoulder, shooting at the dogs, scaring them off. After the last one ran away, the man asked if I was hurt. I took a quick look at myself and the pig, and discovered we only had a few scratches. "It seems that both of us are fine, except for these small scratches on my arms. My pig is scared but is not hurt. Thank you for helping us." The man smiled slightly, "Good. Be careful and always watchful. There are many dangers out here." He walked away from me and returned to the other soldiers. I turned toward home, physically drained.

The days melted into one another. Sometimes there were weeks when life was mundane without all the fighting. Some days were actually boring. Our nerves would have time to relax and we focused all our attention on the family fishing business. Often we would not see other people for days when we were out in the jungle, since usually, it was only the three of us children together at the ocean-side house.

For fun, Phi, Thùy and I would play card games, such as Black Jack, and a Chinese card game called Bai Tu' Sac. This game used skinny cards that resembled fingers. It is a difficult game and still one of my favorites. Usually it was Thùy and I who played Bai Tu' Sac, Phi did not like it as much as we did. After our chores were done, such as opening and closing the water gates, checking the fishing nets, and cooking dinner, we would sit outside and play the card games.

Once, when Thùy lost a game of Bai Tu' Sac to me, she began crying and throwing a fit by kicking the dirt and pushing the cards away, because she now had to pay me what she had bet on the game. Father was inside taking a nap after working hard all night. I tried my best to make her be quiet, but once she started her temper tantrum, Thùy would not be consoled. Her cries woke up Father just as I had feared, and he came running outside, screaming at us. He threatened to beat us if we did not let him sleep. Thùy calmed down, and we promised to be quiet. Father went back inside. I looked at Thùy and gave her my most stern big sister look. "Be quiet or we will both be whipped and I will not take a whipping for you." I glared at her.

One day Father surprised us when he showed up at our ocean house carrying a small yellow baby male tiger. It was about as big as a house cat and so sweet. Father had found him in the jungle while traveling to our home. The baby tiger was starved, so I cooked him some rice and put a small amount of sugar in some water to make it sweet for him. I spoon-fed the tiger and grew to love him. It was nice to have a helpless creature need me.

Two weeks later, Mother came to the house and was going to cook crabs for us that night. She had brought some crabs that were still alive and crawling around. The tiger saw the crabs and walked over to one, playfully batting at it. When his paw touched it, the crab swiftly stuck out its claw, grabbing the tiger's stomach. I kicked the crab off and scooped up the tiger and ran away. His belly was bleeding, and he was in obvious pain. I tended to him as best I could, but within a few days, my baby tiger died, most likely from an infection. I was heartbroken. "Did life only bring pain and tears?" I wondered. I buried my tiger in a grave near the house, and for weeks I cried each time I walked by the site. Even to this day, I get sad thinking about him. Love was so fleeting during that time of my life.

As the days passed, the war raged on. Whenever I heard airplanes pass overhead, I nearly became physically ill. If they flew over during the night, I was unable to go back to sleep. I found myself often crying. The stress was enormous. We were frequently without our parents for days and found ourselves worried about every unfamiliar sound coming through the dense jungle.

We had more than soliders to be scared of. One day, when I was eleven years old, my brother Phi was taking a nap after working the night before opening the flood gates when the tide came in and setting the fish nets. Thùy and I were outside. Suddenly, a noise startled me, and I looked up to see two wolves that had sneaked up on us out of the depths of the jungle. We started yelling for Phi to wake up and picked up rocks to throw at the wolves. He ran out to see what all the commotion was about and began screaming at the wolves too. Luckily, they were frightened and turned and ran back into the cover of the trees. We all knew if they had charged us, we had nowhere to go. Our house did not have a front door for us to hide behind. We did not even have our parents on a regular basis to protect us. They were usually several kilometers away at their house.

It seemed there was always some misfortune that we had to deal with. After our wolf scare, we had a mosquito scare. After the three of us had gone to bed, Phi could not sleep because the mosquitoes were ferocious that night. Even with mosquito netting, they still had a way of tormenting us after dark. Phi got up and lit a candle so he could see to kill some of the mosquitoes. Unfortunately, he was careless with the candle and caught the netting on fire. I woke up as he screamed "Fire!" over and over. We got Thùy up, and we ran out of the house as fast as we could. Phi grabbed a can of water that was just outside the front door and ran back in, throwing the water on the burning net. Thankfully, we were able to extinguish the fire, but when it was all over, we were soaked as were our beds. There was no more sleep for us that night. We were able to repair and dry out the house before our parents came for a visit. They never knew their children had nearly burned down their house and set the jungle on fire. We did not see any need to tell them.

We always went barefoot while working in the jungle and wore sandals only at night upon returning home from working the fishing operation. The jungle was unforgiving to shoes. There were so many water holes and large ponds due to the Mekong River and its tributaries that the mud would suck off any shoe I wore. It was easier just to go barefoot. Of course, bare feet are prone to injury while walking over fallen trees and rocks. But because I was still a young and stupid girl, my feet were in danger of being injured because of my careless actions. For instance, once when I was walking along the shore of the river I saw a clam shell. Without thinking, I kicked the shell with my bare foot. The shell sliced my foot open, and the wound became infected. Within a few days, my injury worsened. Mother sent me to Bac Liêu to get the infection cleaned and proper medicine applied. I never kicked a clam shell again, and I grew to respect my feet.

Washing clothes was one of my chores. I washed them by hand in the river, just like I washed my body. We had soap, but the river was salty, so clothes, as well as bodies, never really felt clean. If we happened to have new clothes, which usually occurred only during the New Year celebrations, we washed our new clothes in clean water using powder soap when we were at my grandparents' home. Baths were really special if we had caught rainwater. We used it instead of river water. During droughts, my parents would go into town and buy fresh water and bring it back to our house in the jungle in large containers. We had to use it sparingly in order to make it last as long as possible. But mostly, the fresh water was used for cooking and drinking before we washed with it.

6

On January 31, 1968, a major fight broke out between the North and South Vietnamese, which impacted my life. This battle would become known as the infamous Têt Offensive. Seventy-thousand VC and North Vietnamese soldiers launched an attack against the South Vietnamese and American soldiers during the lunar New Year known as Tet. The VC simultaneously invaded thirteen of the sixteen provincial capitals of the Mekong Delta, including my town, Bac Liêu.

The timing of this battle was critical due to the sacredness of the Tet holiday held by Vietnamese. Tet, which means the first morning of the first day of the lunar New Year, begins in mid-February, and the celebration lasts for seven days. There are many traditions surrounding Tet. A week before it starts, homes are thoroughly cleaned in order to remove bad fortune that may linger from the past year. Families paint their homes to give it a new look, and everyone gets new clothes and shoes. We would sweep the dirt and trash into a corner of the house where it remained until after the holiday. It is believed that if you throw it away, you will have bad luck. Everyone works hard to save money for this holiday because one must pay all debts during this time and resolve differences between family and friends; otherwise, one is destined to have bad luck in the coming year.

During the last three days of Tet, no one works. We play games, go to the movies, wear our new clothes, visit friends, and pray and light incense to Buddha. As a child, I would go with my family to our neighbors' homes and light incense and pray for them. The colors red and yellow are considered good luck omens, so each house had watermelon for its red fruit. My grandmother would also put out yellow flowers for extra luck.

Special foods are cooked for Tet. I remember making sweet rice by mixing mung beans, which were yellow beans, with salt, bacon, and banana leaves. This delicious dish is called Bánh Tét. My mother would stay awake all night to make the sweet rice because she had to keep the pan filled with water while it cooked for hours. The markets were very busy the days leading up to Tet, much like during the Christmas season in America.

On the actual day of Tet, people place small amounts of money in special red envelopes to give away to others throughout the day. The children know these envelopes hold wonderful surprises. Tet is a time of happiness and joy. This was precisely why the VC chose that holiday week to launch such a large and vicious attack. Most people would be in a celebratory mood, eating, drinking, playing and gambling, not on their guard for enemies. No one would be thinking about war.

One of my cousins was a South soldier, a ngūoi lính. He had warned the family of the impending battle. My parents and we three children went to our grandparents' home, where we joined them and several other family members. In anticipation of war, my relatives had dug a big underground shelter behind my grandparents' house that was large enough for all of us to hide in during the anticipated clash. There were fifteen of us who lived in this earthen shelter, including me, my parents and siblings, my grandparents, and eight aunts and uncles.

The shelter was a hole that led down a five foot long tunnel which ended in a circular underground shelter. It did not allow for anyone to stand up; all we could do was sit or lie down. The floor was dirt while the ceiling was comprised of tree branches that were laid across the width of the entrance hole and tied together. We covered the branches with rice husks because they acted as a cushion to protect us from the shelling from tanks and whatever else the enemy rained down on us. Rice husks are the protective hard covering of the rice grain. The husks are often used to insulate buildings because they do not absorb water. So when artillery struck the husks, the impact was lessened and we were safe from major damage. We took a few oil lamps with us so we would not have to sit in the darkness after the sun went down. Grandmother would check for snakes in our shelter each morning once the daylight filtered through the rice husks. All we could do was pray to Buddha and sleep.

The fighting came upon us quickly, and it was fierce. There had been no time to gather food or water supplies. Day after day we heard the sounds of guns and people screaming above us. We were so afraid we would be discovered and shot by soldiers looming over us. After four days had passed, we realized there was stillness above us, not a sound of war could be heard. We crept out, one at a time, grabbed some food and water, and returned to the shelter for another three days. At the end of the week, we came out for good, slowly peeking out at a world we did not recognize. There were body parts in trees, on houses, in the streets. I stood there looking around in horror. It was a nightmare scene. The adults found baskets and began the grim task of collecting the various body parts. One person found a leg on the roof of my grandparents' home. The townspeople cleaned away the destruction of war from Bac Liêu. Many people had died for no rational reason. The body parts were buried in a mass grave outside of town.

A few days later, the Viet Cong asked Father to attend a meeting they were having in the jungle. He went only because to refuse invited death. However, he also knew that attending the meeting invited death if the South soldiers found out he went. There was no winning regardless of the decision. When Father was leaving the house I asked him where he was going. He told me it was none of my business and that he would be back later that night. I knew not to press Father for details but I did sense he was nervous. He and Mother spoke quietly to each other where we children could not hear him. Mother began wringing her hands like she did when she was upset or scared. Father put a hand on her shoulder as if calming her.

Even though he told me to stay home, I secretly followed Father when he left that night. I had always been curious and somewhat independent but it seemed that whatever Father was about to do this particular night was very important and I needed to know what was happening. I knew I was taking a big risk but decided to take the chance. If trouble was coming to our family, I wanted to know so I could get my mother and siblings out of the house and hide them in the jungle.

I hid some distance away, behind a very large tree that had thick vegetation growing around the base. I saw several soldiers standing around a large tree. Some were quietly smoking cigarettes while others were talking and laughing. What appeared to be the leaders of the group spoke up and told the group to listen. Father was standing near the outside of the group looking uncomfortable in the midst of all these Communists. He shifted his weight back and forth in a rocking motion. I could sense his unease. My heart was beating wildly with fear of being discovered. I was terrified and wondered why I had felt the need to follow Father. The VC had a large map hanging from tree limbs they pointed at as they discussed various attack strategies and planned their escape routes. I knew I was witnessing a very serious and secretive meeting. I was not certain why Father was brought into the group and guessed he was given instructions on how to help the soldiers escape from the South soldiers. After the recent Tết Offensive the VC had lost nearly 32,000 of their soldiers and they did not want to lose any more.

Later that year, when I was around twelve years old, my aunt, Tám Út, finally visited me in our jungle home. It was strange to think that at one time we considered ourselves twin sisters. Odd, we looked nothing alike now. Tám Út came out for the day to see how our family lived. As luck would have it, that day a helicopter flew low and directly over us. We were inside cleaning the house and finishing up some other mundane chores when suddenly I heard helicopter blades—whump, whump, whump—steadily growing louder. As if she did not know there was a war going on, Tám Út wanted to run outside and look at it. But I knew better than that. "No, Tám Út, stay inside. They are trying to discover if there are any people here. Lie on the floor and do not move," I shouted at her. I grabbed her arm, pulling her down next to me. From my position,

I could see through the front door opening and looked toward the sky. I could make out one gunner holding onto his machinegun in the helicopter. There were two machineguns poking out the open side and soldiers sitting behind each one. Gunfire erupted all around the house. I grabbed my sister and told her to lie down on the floor. Then the pig ran inside and lay next to us. My heroic pig stayed close to me until the day we sold him at market.

The soldiers circled our house several times. We thought they would never leave. All of a sudden, a loud explosion came from the front yard, showering the house with dirt and leaves. The South soldiers had thrown a grenade in our yard, trying to get us to run outside. If we had, we would have been killed by the machinegun. We did not move, hardly daring to breathe. We lay there, shaking, wondering if in the next moment the house would blow up or if we would be struck by the machinegun through our roof and walls. Tám Út was quietly moaning, shivering from fear.

How hardened I had become, I thought. While this whole incident had been unsettling, I still saw it as just that, an incident. There had been a time not too long ago that I would have wanted to run screaming from the house, just like Tám Út had wanted to do. After what seemed an eternity but was probably only a few moments, the helicopter flew away, apparently deciding there was no one in the house and left to go scare another jungle family. We got up, looked outside and saw a huge hole right past the front door. I knew the helicopter had been manned by Vietnamese soldiers for I had seen their faces. But the helicopter had been an American-made machine. I quickly learned what we had experienced was a common practice of war. Soldiers would shoot around a house, throw an explosive device and see if anyone came running out. If they did, the soldiers would shoot them. Tám Út left for Bac Liêu as soon as she could that same day. She had learned our lives were not exotic nor a picnic, but rather, we struggled to simply survive.

About a year later, around late 1969 or early 1970, Tám Út returned for another visit. Perhaps she had to prove to us and herself that she was not scared to be out here any more than the rest of us. Thùy and I had a small transistor radio we listened to at night. We could tune into a radio station that played the music of the latest Vietnamese singers. When we listened, we momentarily forgot we had been living in a jungle for years. We could pretend to have hope for a brighter, more civilized future.

When Tám Út arrived, she did not like the station we had tuned in. She made fun of the singer who was on at that moment and demanded we change to another station. Thùy and I fiercely clung to the one thing we had absolute control over, our radio. Our lives were dictated by Father, the Viet Cong, the South soldiers, the seafood season; but this radio, well, it represented to us everything we did not have. We stood our ground against Tám Út, refusing to change the dial. This was the person who I at one time could not imagine being separated from, my twin. Now, she could go away and never come back, I thought. The radio station would not be changed. Tám Út became so mad at us that she left the house right then and walked the two hours back to Bac Liêu by herself. It is amazing how brave an irate woman can be, even in the midst of war.

The VC were known to kidnap people at night, blindfold them, and take them into the jungle. When I was thirteen, the Assistant Mayor of Bac Liêu was kidnapped in that manner. This man was fifty-two years old and had a family. He was taken to the jungle where the VC kept him for a few days, and then he was brought to our home, the one nearest the ocean. They arrived some time after midnight. We children were alone and stunned to see the group of soldiers and their captive. "Now what do we do?" we wondered. The VC told me to cook some rice and give it to the man. He remained blindfolded. While he ate the soldiers kept promising him he would not be killed and would be set free once they returned to Bac Liêu. He appeared to be more at ease, eating the rice, talking to the VC like they were old friends. "Yes," the soldiers said, "you will not be harmed. Eat the food and relax." "Would they really let him return to his family?" I thought.

They left after about an hour, which was the strangest hour of my life. Here I was, surrounded by Viet Cong soldiers who had kidnapped the Assistant Mayor, feeding the man rice while we all wondered if he would be dead soon. My grandfather later told me what happened next. Upon returning to Bac Liêu, the VC placed the man in an area not too far from his neighborhood and home. It was a common area where the town's men often met with one another to drink and catch up on the latest news. The soldiers then went to all the man's neighbors, including Grandfather, waking them up, one house at a time, demanding they attend a meeting with the Assistant Mayor. Grandfather and all the other men left their houses as instructed and gathered around the kidnapped man, who was still blindfolded. He had no idea there were nearly thirty of his friends and neighbors standing around him. He was still chatting blindly with his captors, believing he was about to be set free.

Suddenly, one VC stepped forward into the middle of the circle, and started speaking about the Assistant Mayor. He told those who had gathered lies about the man, how he had conspired with the Americans to do all of them harm. The Assistant Mayor then began to realize what was happening. The VC was trying to get his friends to believe he was a traitor. The Assistant Mayor's face became tense, but he was too intimidated to speak up on his own behalf. All he could do was sit there and listen, not sure who else was around him. While the soldier was talking, another soldier standing behind the Assistant Mayor quickly drew out a sword and cut off his head. Everyone stood there in shock. Grandfather said he could not believe what he had just seen. This man, this city leader, who had been casually talking with his captors only moments earlier, now had his head lying on the ground next to his legs. Slowly, the men left when the VC said they could go back home. Everyone knew that it could be them or someone they loved the next time.

That same year, 1970, I had my first and only experience with Agent Orange. This poison was dropped on the jungle near Bac Liêu. We had no idea what it was at first. Then the jungle started dying, stretching from the South China Sea to about a mile inland. Luckily, our house in the jungle was not affected, but many people in the city became sick. They began coughing, having runny noses, and many babies were born deformed. I saw children who were born with their fingers fused together and some whose legs were bent and crooked. It was terribly sad to see.

A few months later, two of my uncles, my father's younger brothers, Quang and Tinh, shocked the family when they joined the Communists and became VC soldiers. Both were sent away from Bac Liêu by their commanders. My grandparents were terrified the nguôi lính would find out their sons were fighting on the opposing side and they in turn would be harmed as an example for other families. Some neighbors found out about my uncles' actions and promptly starting demanding money from my grandparents. They promised to keep the secret in exchange for a handsome amount of money. My grandparents complied, feeling that they had no choice.

Uncle Quang was married and had three children. After leaving Bac Liêu, he settled in Ca Mau, the same town where my parents had lived when I was very young. Due to the large number of Communists that had infiltrated that area, the Americans began bombing Ca Mau daily. Quang dug an underground shelter for his family in the jungle for them to hide in during the intense bombing raids while he was away fighting with his unit. During one bombing incident his wife, children and mother-in-law sought refuge in the shelter for a few days.

After the fighting quieted down, his mother-in-law and 13-year old daughter decided to return to the family home in Ca Mau to retrieve some medicine and blankets. His wife and other two children, a 2-year old son and 16-year old daughter, remained in the shelter. While his mother-in-law and youngest daughter were in town, the Americans dropped napalm down the mouth of the shelter, killing the three who had remained in what they thought was a safe place. When his mother-in-law returned to the shelter after the fire had extinguished itself, she found that her daughter's face had been clawed by the two-year old boy as he had tried to get out of the fire pit. His mother-in-law and daughter found Uncle Quang in the city to where he had been sent by his commander and delivered the devastating news of the death of his beloved wife and two children.

A year later, Quang remarried, and he and his new wife had a son and a daughter. He had been promoted up the ranks and was now a general in the Communist army. During a bombing in 1972, he was hiding with his second family in a jungle underground shelter. The bomb's impact broke both of Quang's legs. His wife took him to Bac Liêu for medical care where he was hospitalized.

Going to Bac Liêu was very dangerous for him because he was a Viet Cong general. But, as my grandparents later learned, his wife knew that and deliberately placed Quang in danger because she had a boyfriend with whom she wanted to make a life. My grandparents pleaded with her to move Quang to a hospital in another town where he would be safer, but his wife would not relent.

Finally, Grandmother convinced Quang's doctor to release him to her care so she could take him to her home. However, the day Quang was released from the hospital, the doctor injected poison into his legs, which made the flesh fall off. Grandmother paid large sums of money for Chinese medicine to help her son, but it was too late. The gangrene had spread throughout his body and he died a few weeks later. Not too long after his death, his wife married her boyfriend. She took Uncle Quang's son and daughter away from my grandparents. His surviving daughter from his first wife had remained with her dead mother's mother in Ca Mau.

My uncle Tinh, who had also joined the Communist Army, married and had two sons. During his tenure as a soldier, his commander sent him and four other soldiers to fight in a small town about an hour away from Bac Liêu to fight. As they were leaving the town, they became lost and could not find their way out of the city. As they searched in the night for the road that would take them out of the town, they were surprised by South soldiers and all five were killed. My uncle and his four comrades were tossed into a mass grave and buried together.

In 1972 the South soldiers had a camp a few miles from our middle home in the jungle. I was 15 years old at that time. Phi was at the ocean house with our parents while Thùy and I were in this middle house, about three miles away from my brother and parents. At about three o'clock one afternoon, Phi came to check on us. After being reassured we were fine, Phi left to return to the ocean house around seven o'clock that night.

He had walked about twenty yards from where I stood in the house, when suddenly a firefight broke out from nowhere. Gunfire sounding like popcorn popping, smacked through the air, and hand grenades were thrown out from among the trees toward our direction. Phi jumped into the lake to avoid being shot. I looked out the door at about the time he jumped and I thought he had been hit. A bullet whizzed by my head, and I fell to the floor to save my own life. I risked another look outside and saw an injured soldier and Phi get out of the water and run together into the jungle. Phi appeared to be all right. I grabbed Thùy by the hand and we ran after them.

We met up in the jungle and together the three of us made our way to our parents at the ocean house. We were exhausted. At about nine o'clock that night, the mother of the injured soldier who had helped Phi escape the firefight came to our house and begged Father to help her find her son. He agreed and they went out looking for him. They found her son hiding in the jungle near the middle house.

The next day, I was sent into town to sell seafood (money still had to be made no matter how close to death we had come the day before), and I ran into Father's best friend. He warned me that the South soldiers were coming to arrest Father because they believed he had helped the VC with the attack the day before. I learned the VC had attacked the South soldiers' camp and kidnapped one of their generals. The South soldiers believed my father had told the Communists where their camp had been hidden since it was among the trees so near our home. I rushed back and told Father he was about to be arrested. "It is serious this time," I said; "they think you helped the VC kidnap a general." Father and Mother fled to our grandparents' home in Bac Liêu and moved around among other family members' houses for the next two weeks.

As predicted, the soldiers came to our house looking for Father. Thùy, Phi and I were left at the house to face the soldiers' questions. The soldiers searched for Father for more than a week. They were furious about Father's supposed treason. We gave them our standard response, "I do not know," whenever we were asked where Father had gone or if he had aided the Communists. We were terrified the soldiers would make an example out of one or all of us in order to bring our parents out of hiding. I could not get the image out of my mind of the Assistant Mayor's head lying on the ground. I knew the kinds of terror these soldiers were capable of inflicting.

One day, while Father and Mother were still in hiding, Phi and I had caught about two hundred pounds of fish and shrimp near our ocean house. It was a long day of hard work. A group of soldiers came by the house, leading two prisoners to the jail in Bac Liêu. The soldiers, who were still looking for Father, began searching our house under the pretense of looking for our seafood so they could take it for their dinner. They searched under the bed, as if we hid fish and shrimp there. We knew exactly what, rather who, they were looking for. When they finally decided to take all of our food and leave, Phi asked the group's leader if they would leave a little bit of fish for our dinner, otherwise we had nothing to eat. The leader began screaming at Phi, calling him a Communist. We just cowered in the corner, afraid to make eye contact.

Before we could react, Phi was tied up and became their third prisoner. Phi and I were crying, begging the soldiers to leave him alone, promising them he was most certainly not a dirty Communist, but all of our tears and pleadings went unheard. Phi was led away to Bac Liêu to be put in jail along with the other two prisoners. Phi, who was 17 years old, was placed with other prisoners who were much older.

The next day, Thùy and I ran through the jungle to Bac Liêu to find our parents and tell them what happened to Phi. They were still fugitives due to the kidnapping accusations. After about two weeks, the family raised enough money to buy Phi out of jail. We paid about 300,000 đồng, which was enough money at that time to build a house.

Eventually, our great-uncle asked the soldiers to grant Father permission to return home to care for his children. Uncle reassured the soldiers that Father had nothing to do with the battle in which several South soldiers were injured and killed and the general was kidnapped. Finally the soldiers' commander agreed Father could come out of hiding, but he would have to pay a large amount of bail. No wonder we never had much money, it was always being spent paying for someone's bail.

In addition to stealing the seafood we caught, the soldiers would toss hand grenades into the lake to blow up the fish. The dead fish and shrimp would float to the top of the lake making it easy to get them, but it also left a mess in the water with fish parts floating around. Since seafood was my family's livelihood, it was essential to keep the water clean and not polluted with dead fish. Once the soldiers took their catch, Father would make us clean up the remainder of the carcasses. The mess was unbelievable and took all day.

A few months later I saw some Viet Cong soldiers bury land mines near our house in the jungle during the night. Before sunrise we heard several South soldiers walking close by the house, so Father and I ran to hide underneath a large tree. I had a dog that followed us, and when the soldiers got within earshot, that dog started barking at Father, giving away our hiding place. I hit the dog, chasing him off so that Father would not be spotted by the soldiers. About then four soldiers walked on the buried land mines and were blown up. It was the most peculiar thing to see a body become something less than human in a flash. Luckily for us, the mines distracted the soldiers from pursuing what our dog had barked at—us.

7

The war continued throughout 1972. We were on edge, not knowing what would happen at any given moment. One of those "moments" occurred for Father on an otherwise quiet day as he was walking through the jungle returning home from tending to the fishing nets. He saw a group of South soldiers confronting two men ahead of him. He crept closer and was careful to remain covered by the dense foliage. He realized the two men were the Communist tax collector and his assistant. Since the Vietnamese people had to pay taxes to both the North and South governments during the war years, the Communist tax collector was out making his rounds among the jungle dwellers such as my family. This tax collector had shared drinks with Father and seemed to be a very nice man.

One of the soldiers in the group had started his military career as a VC soldier but had recently left his Communist troop and joined up with the South Republic army. Father saw the two tax collectors talking rapidly and bowing low when suddenly unprovoked the soldiers shot the men. The tax collector was seriously wounded, while his assistant was not hurt as badly. The assistant held the book with the names of the citizens who had paid taxes to the Communists and the amounts they had each paid, and it included Father's name. The assistant ran away carrying the book with him. The tax collector lay on the ground and apparently pretended to be dead. As the soldiers approached him, the former VC soldier recognized the tax collector and told the others who he was. This infuriated all the soldiers because this man was taking money from the people who should have been paying the South Vietnamese regime. One soldier stepped out of the line of men and walked over to the tax collector, and apparently believing the Communist official was dead, took out his machete and cut off the man's head. Before death claimed him, the man thrashed around until his life's blood left him. The soldiers threw the head and body into the river and left the area.

Father ran home after the soldiers disappeared into the jungle and told Mother what he had seen. My parents knew the tax collector's girlfriend, who lived in Bac Liêu, so they went to town to tell her what had happened. The girlfriend came back to the jungle with my parents since she was afraid the soldiers would find and kill her because of her relationship with a VC tax collector. The next day the woman asked Father to help her retrieve the body so she could give it a proper burial. Father and Mother agreed to help and the three of them returned to the river where the head and body had been tossed. When they saw the parts were stuck in the trees, Father became concerned the soldiers had planted bombs in either the head or the body that would explode when touched. It was a common practice to place booby traps on bodies so that others would be killed when the body was moved.

Father found a long stick and used it to push the remains then ran backward as fast as he could. No explosion occurred. After several pushes and jabs, the three of them collected the parts. The face had already been eaten by the fish and was unrecognizable, its features were swollen and purple. If Father had not known who the man had been, it would not have been possible to identify him. Father began to talk to the head telling it how sorry he was they would not be able to drink and talk to each other anymore. A sudden gush of blood came out of the neck as if in response to Father's words. Father and Mother helped the distraught girlfriend bury her sweetheart by the river.

Both sides, the VC and the South soldiers, committed atrocities against ordinary citizens. The Communists were more likely to tell us how bad the South soldiers were, while the South tended to put us in jail, causing us to use all of our money for bail. They did this to Father several times. The VC also used jails; however, theirs were underground. They would dig a deep hole that was about thirty yards wide, and the only access was through a tunnel. The VC would place nearly thirty people in those underground jails and then cover the hole with a solid metal top which prevented the prisoners from seeing outside and caused the air to become stale. Every day someone died in those jails, and the dead bodies were removed by the other prisoners. Those who had survived another day were taken out to work.

Once the VC released a prisoner, the South soldiers would in turn place the newly freed man in another prison for four or five months to determine if he had been brainwashed into joining the Communists and becoming a traitor. When the South soldiers felt assured that he was not a traitor, then the former prisoner of war was allowed to return home.

It was not unusual for the Communists to recruit young boys to become soldiers. The VC once approached my brother Phi about joining their cause. They promised him greatness and told him how honorable it was to be a Communist soldier, a soldier in the North Vietnamese Army. But Phi refused to join, unlike another young boy, whose grandmother was my grandparents neighbor. This boy was eleven years old and lived with his maternal grandmother because both of his parents had committed suicide the previous year. No one ever discussed the events that had led up to their deaths, but we all knew how devastated the boy had been when it happened. He was exactly the type of person the VC could easily persuade, which they did.

A few weeks after the boy had left his grandmother's home, Phi and I saw him carrying a big gun and dressed in the VC uniform and hat. He was so naïve to not realize the South soldiers would arrest him for being a Communist which, of course, they did. They held him in jail for five weeks until finally letting him out after his grandmother pleaded for him and paid money for his release. This boy never returned to the Communists. Probably his stay in jail with other older, more hardened men made him want to remain within the safety of his grandmother's home.

Even in the middle of a war, there were the normal parent-child conflicts that happened. Around the time of Tết in 1972, when we were fifteen, my aunt Tám Út and I decided to change our hair-styles. We both had very long and dark silky hair, which we found difficult to keep clean and brushed. Thus, we wanted a short hair-style that was more easily managed. We went to a salon in Bac Liêu and had our hair cut very short and a curly permanent applied. We thought we looked beautiful and stylish. Tám Út and I returned to Grandfather's house to show off our new hair styles. We did not expect to receive what we got.

Grandfather took one look at us and became so angry I almost did not recognize him. He ordered Tám Út to lie on the bed on her stomach and then beat her on the buttocks with a stick. She cried and begged him to stop, promising she would never cut her hair again. But Grandfather was enraged and would not stop hitting her. One of his friends heard Tám Út's screams, and he came inside the house to see what was happening. This older man quickly realized what was happening and knew Grandfather was taking the punishment too far. He grabbed Grandfather's wrist and yelled. "Stop, that is enough. She is your daughter, and you should forgive her. Besides, she looks pretty. Her hair is not that bad." Grandfather turned around, looked at his friend, and dropped the stick. We had been stupid to not realize the tremendous error of what we had done. In Vietnamese families only the parents have the right to cut their children's hair; otherwise, the family risks having bad luck. My father and grandfather took this superstition seriously, as we belatedly found out.

I ran out of the house once I realized Tám Út was safe from any further beating because I knew Father would be angry at me, just as Tám Út's father had been. I went to the neighbor's house and stayed there for two days. I would sneak around the area, spying on my family trying to determine just how much trouble I was in. I saw Father walking around the neighborhood looking for me and heard him calling my name and asking people if they had seen me. Fortunately, the friends who hid me knew about my father's temper and kept my secret. Once, Father came close to the house in which I was hiding, so I ran and hid in a closet, which was more of a tall airless box. It was sweltering inside. After about thirty minutes, I peeked out. Father was gone. Thankfully, I stepped out of the box and took some deep breaths of fresh air. That night I saw Mother walk near the house, so I gathered all my courage and approached her. She looked at me and said, "I have been worried about you. You need to come home." "But when can I, Mother? You know how Father can be; he will beat me like Grandfather beat Tám Út." She shook her head, "He is still mad at you, but I do not think he is as angry now as he was two days ago. You come home tomorrow and everything will be all right. Besides, it is the New Year's celebration."

That night I lay awake worried sick. Should I go home? I knew I had to go eventually, so I decided I might as well face the consequences and have some peace. The next day I quietly slipped back into my grandparents' house where my parents were staying. Father was there and looked up at me as I walked in. He did not say a word or acknowledge me for a few days, which was fine with me. He was preoccupied with drinking and celebrating the New Year with all the Tết festivities. I did not cut my hair for years after that. It seems to be an odd twist of fate that I grew up to be a beautician.

In the spring of 1972, a few months after the haircut incident, the fighting between the South soldiers and the Communists intensified. The soldiers were shooting at each other near all of our homes, both in the jungle, along the river, and in Bac Liêu. Bombs dropped from airplanes often exploded nearby. Once when I was staying in town, a fight erupted between the two sides. People began fleeing on foot through the streets of Bac Liêu, fearing their homes would be bombed and that approaching soldiers would enter the houses and kill anyone found there. Instead those fleeing, terrified people were gunned down on the streets, often leaving small children trapped alive under their bodies. Children wandered around the city, alone and crying, because their parents were lying dead on the streets. The dead people were tossed into a mass grave dug outside of town.

One night while staying at my grandparents' house, I was awakened at 3:00 a.m. by the sound of artillery. I jumped from bed and began crawling on the floor like a baby. Grandmother saw me and said, "Stay down, there is shooting all around the house, keep your head down." I was shaking uncontrollably. This was one of the more aggressive battles I had ever heard. Suddenly, there was a thumping sound on the roof. We then smelled smoke and realized the house had been set on fire. The smoke quickly became thick, and the heat of the flames filled the room. My grandparents, aunt, and I scrambled to our feet and grabbed buckets of water, throwing them on the flames. We were able to extinguish the fire quickly and cowered down again on the soggy floor amid the smoky smell. We learned later the thumping noise we had heard had been a parachute landing on the roof that had a flare attached to it. This was often a war strategy to illuminate the sky for the soldiers.

The next day the shooting stopped for a few hours. We heard people crying out for their loved ones. They were asking if anyone had seen their family members; even worse, I witnessed people weeping over the bodies of their sons, husbands, and fathers. Others were shouting that the man of the house had been taken away by the soldiers. Many of those were never seen again. It was a very sad time since so many innocent people lost their homes and families. Numerous people lost parts of themselves as well, like their arms and legs. To this day, my nightmares are filled with people who have to crawl because they have no legs and no one will help them.

I turned 16 in 1973. One day at the ocean house by myself, I was puttering around doing my usual chores, tending to the water gates and cleaning the house. I was outside when I heard someone approaching through the jungle. I grew tense, as I often was, and saw a young Communist soldier emerge from the jungle into the clearing. He asked me for some food. He looked so young and thin, his clothing dirty and torn. I fed him from the meager supplies I had at that moment, and he was grateful for it. We did not talk to each other while he ate, but merely watched one another from a distance. After he finished eating, he left and headed back into the jungle. I went on about my business without another thought of him.

The next day I went to Bac Liêu to sell the fish we had caught that week. A crowd was gathered around something in the middle of the town, drawing me closer with curiosity. I gasped when I saw the body. It was the young soldier I had fed the day before. I asked the person standing next to me what had happened to him and was told he had been shot and killed the night before by the nguoi lính. Then his body had been tied to the back of a truck and was dragged through town for everyone to see. Another mother had lost a son this day, I thought. So much pain and sadness . . . for what? I wondered.

While the nguoi lính were viciously killing the Viet Cong soldiers, the VC asked Father to help them in their fight against the South soldiers. He was asked to hang white clothing in an obvious position whenever South soldiers were in the area of any of the three houses we had in the jungle. This would alert the VC to the nguoi lính presence and they would be able to kill or capture the enemy or to slip away without being detected. Father did as he was asked and made it appear as if the signal clothing was merely laundry hung out to dry. I was very much against helping the Communists and refused to comply with their request. Even though Father asked me to help the VC, I did not obey him. I could be as stubborn as my father, and he had begun to realize that side of me. We quietly agreed to disagree on this subject, and he never pressured me to do the VC bidding. I was terrified the South soldiers would discover what Father was doing and torture and kill him, as well as all of my family. Fortunately, they never did.

It was about this time in my life, from my early teens until I was eighteen that my brother, sister and I moved back and forth from the jungle to my grandparents' home in town. Whenever Father needed us to help with the fishing operation, he would come get us and take us to the jungle. We would remain there for three days to a week at a time, completing our fishing chores. Sometimes there could be several months before our return to the jungle, depending on the seasons. We were with our grandparents during the dry seasons and returned to the jungle when the wet season came back around. The time with our grandparents was a respite from the harshness of the jungle life and war.

8

The war finally ended in 1975 when the Communists over ran the country, defeating the Army of the Republic of Vietnam. South Vietnam was no more. In April the capitol city of South Vietnam, Saigon, was taken over and renamed Ho Chi Minh City, after the dead Communist leader. I was eighteen and had lost my childhood. I had grown up in an environment of death and suffering.

The whole economic structure of Vietnam faced serious problems. Once the American aid was removed from our country, money was in short supply. The forests in the southern part of the "new" Vietnam had been devastated by napalm and Agent Orange, and consequently rice farms were in ruins. Northern Vietnam found itself inundated with millions of refugees, many of whom were former soldiers, drug addicts, and prostitutes. Hundreds of thousands of impoverished north people were sent by the Communists to live in the south, creating overcrowding in Bac Liêu.

Many of Bac Liêu's citizens were forced to move from the city to the jungle by the North Vietnamese who took over the businesses and homes formerly owned by the South Vietnamese people. Most of us were displaced to smaller homes or the jungle.

We had no choice but to start working for the new government. Landowners had their land taken away from them and became mere laborers who were paid a daily wage. The Communists seized almost all of Father's land, leaving him only two of his original seven miles of property. They placed five families from the capitol city of Hanoi on the land that was taken from him. Father received no compensation for his land or all the work he had done to develop the land or his fishing operation over the past several years. It was just gone, taken away. Father was hired by the new government to cut trees in the jungle to open up the land and clear out the trees that had died when Agent Orange was dropped. Also more open land reduced the possibility of those who did not agree with the Communist way of life constructing hideouts.

Only people who worked for the Communists had the authority to cut the trees. However, many South Vietnamese would go into the jungle and illegally cut them in order to sell the wood. One day Father saw five small children cutting wood in the area he was working. He made them come with him to our jungle home where I was working. Each one of them had a sling filled with wood they carried on their backs. It was a heavy burden for children.

Father called out to me and told me to watch the children while he went to bring the Communists soldiers back to arrest them. After Father left, the children started crying and looked very scared. "These children were too young to be taken to jail. They are only five to ten years old," I thought. I remembered the days when I and my siblings had been just as scared of being arrested or even killed by the Communists. My heart began to break, hearing their sobs. "Shhh," I said to them. "It will be fine. They will just take you back to town and tell you not to cut the trees without the proper permits. Everything will be all right." I tried to soothe their fears, but it was no use; they did not believe me. I understood their distrust of my words. No one could predict what the Communists would do in order to set an example for everyone else. They were now in power and often abused their authority. Just as Father feared not turning the children in, the local authorities may have also feared not enforcing the law strictly—even on children.

The more I thought about it, the more determined I became to ensure these children would not be handed over to the soldiers. "Go, go quickly, and do not come back to this area again or I will let them arrest you." I shooed them away and watched as they quickly disappeared among the trees.

About an hour later, Father returned with some soldiers in a Jeep. "Where are the children?" he demanded when he saw they were gone.

I just stood there without speaking. The soldiers began yelling at me, threatening to arrest me in place of the missing children. "If you are willing to go to jail on their behalf, we will be glad to take you," they barked at me. I remained silent. I knew it would be easier for me than those children to spend time in jail. I was willing to take that chance. After a verbal berating by both Father and the soldiers, they finally left angrily. Father glared at me but did not say anything else. He knew I could be as stubborn as he was. We continued with our chores, not saying anything to each other about the incident. I hope Father was privately pleased with my bravery facing down the soldiers.

By 1978 the majority of businesses and merchandise belonged to the government. In their attempt to further exercise control over the country, the Communists deported numerous rich South families from Ho Chi Minh City to Bac Liêu. They were stripped of their wealth and uprooted from their life of luxury in the city to a life of poverty in the more rural Mekong Delta area.

Many business owners who lost everything to the new regime committed suicide. They could not bear to see all their hard work devoured by the North Vietnamese who had pushed them out of the way as if they were a nuisance. Some of the Bac Liêu families who had been forced to retreat into the jungle would often go into town after midnight and knock on the doors of their former homes now occupied by the North Vietnamese. When they answered the knocking, the North people were kidnapped and taken into the jungle to be left abandoned and scared after the former Bac Liêu citizens threatened them if they did not leave and return to Ho Chi Minh City. There was much unrest during this time.

Farmers were told what crop to plant and how much to produce. The new government then bought the rice or other product at a very low rate that was not profitable at all. This hard work for no profit kept farmers from growing any more than simply enough for their own use. Rice farmers, like Grandfather, could only keep twenty percent of their crop, with the rest going to the government. Rations grew scarce, and many people began to starve.

The Communists also changed out the money so that people who had been wealthy in the South before and during the war, like my grandparents, no longer had any money. The government would offer to exchange the old money for only a small amount of the new money, thereby depleting their wealth. The nation's money supply was changed a few times a year to prevent people from stockpiling it. Rich people would ask poor people to help them make the money exchange for a small fee so they could get more exchanged, and reduce their loss. But most rich people quickly became poor. It was very difficult for them to accept the new lower status in life, and suicides were not unusual. The Communists kept telling us they wanted everyone to be equal and to get rid of the different classes of people. But we quickly realized they only wanted to have poor people who were dependent on the government.

Not long after the war ended, my sister Thùy went to visit Aunt Lai, my father's younger sister, in Ho Chi Minh City. Lai, who was my number five aunt, was nine years older than I and eleven years older than Thùy. Lai had married and moved to the former Saigon years earlier where she worked as a tailor. She was now a divorcee with three children. Her former husband was the father of two of the children, while the third child, a daughter, had been conceived when Lai had become involved with a rich married man. Thùy agreed to come and help her care for the children. Thùy thought she would be there for a short while, maybe a few months at most, staying until gasoline was not so scarce and she could ride the bus back home to Bac Lieu. But the end of the war made gas difficult to obtain, and it was very expensive if you were lucky to find it. She had no idea her visit would last two years.

In 1977 I grew worried about Thùy because I had difficulty communicating with her. She was not available by phone since Lai did not have a telephone and she rarely wrote back when I sent letters to her. I decided I would go to Ho Chi Minh City, find her and see what was going on. I bought a bus ticket and took off on the seven hour trip. I showed up at Lai's house unannounced one afternoon, which did not seem to make Lai very happy at all. Thùy was ecstatic to see me. We hugged each other tightly, and I saw tears in her eyes. Thùy asked me if I wanted to see the city, after putting down my suitcase. I said yes, and we went for a walk, leaving Lai at home.

I asked Thùy why I had not heard from her and why she had remained in Ho Chi Minh City so long. She told me that Lai would not let her leave and had kept her a virtual prisoner. Lai would not give my sister any money for bus fare and made her stay at the house all the time so she could not call out for help. Lai was determined not to let a free babysitter get away from her. We crafted a plan to leave that night after our aunt went to bed.

I had enough money to buy our bus tickets back to Bac Liêu. We visited with Lai that evening and played with her children until bedtime. We said our good nights and went upstairs. Hours passed until we felt confident that Lai had gone to sleep. Around midnight, once the house had grown quiet, we crept downstairs. We quickly changed out of our pajamas and left through the front door. I locked the door behind us and tried to quietly slip the key back under the door. Every sound seemed amplified. We hurried away from the house and caught a ride on a pedi-taxi. The man who drove the makeshift bicycle taxi took us for a long ride. Two hours later we finally arrived at the bus station. The station was closed until morning but there were already several people lying on the floor waiting for their chance to buy a ticket to somewhere.

I asked some of them how long they had been there and they told me three days. They had been sleeping on the ground waiting on the bus. Thùy and I remained at the station that night and the next day, all the while keeping a watchful eye out for Aunt Lai. At about five o'clock on the second morning, people started forming a line to buy tickets, so we joined them. The line was long and people began pushing each other out of the way. We were at the back of the line that extended outside of the station.

A lady approached us and said we had to pay her to get on the bus since she owned the bus company; otherwise we could not get a ticket. I did not believe her, but Thùy was worried Lai would find us and told me to give her our money. I gave her all the money we had and she told us to get on the bus. We climbed aboard and sat down feeling relieved. After about ten minutes another person approached us and demanded the money for the tickets. I told him we had already paid a lady for our tickets, and he said, "Well, you have not paid me yet, and I am the one who owns this bus." I looked around for the lady who took our money, but she was gone, just as I had feared. We had no money left, so I sold my earrings to a man sitting next to us, which gave us enough to buy a second set of tickets. I was so angry at being tricked and very upset I had to give up my jewelry. But Thùy and I wanted to go home. It was worth the price we paid just to get out of this dreadful city.

Lai showed up in Bac Liêu within a few days after discovering we had left. She began screaming at family members that she needed Thùy to come back and take care of her children. We hid at Father's house in the jungle for a week until Lai left town. To our surprise, she took Phi back to Ho Chi Minh City with her, where he stayed for a month. We could not believe he actually went with her. However, he was resourceful enough to return home without having to be rescued.

Two years later Aunt Lai was arrested for allegedly hiring a man to kill her married boyfriend's wife. We found that even though Lai had a child with this man, his wife refused to give him a divorce. In fact, the wife offered Lai money to leave her husband alone, but Lai, stubborn as she was, wanted this rich man and refused to end the affair. Then one day, his wife was found stabbed to death. Lai and the husband were accused by the dead woman's children of hiring another man to do the killing. All three of them were arrested, but only Lai remained in jail, after the two men posted bond. Their charges were soon dismissed. About six months later, Grandfather was told by the Communist police that Lai had hanged herself in her cell. However, the family learned from other prisoners housed with her that the Communists had shot Lai to death. Her three children were sent to Bac Liêu and raised by my grandparents. Lai was domineering and a bit strange, but we certainly did not wish for this type of ending to befall her.

After Phi returned from Ho Chi Minh City, the Communists convinced Father to send him to Ca Mau to join the army for one year. Father thought it was a good idea for Phi to be a soldier so the Communists would like our family. But instead of becoming a soldier, Phi was used as a laborer by the government to cut wood alongside hundreds of other people. He stayed for two years, not the one year as had been promised to Father. The Communists lied whenever it gave them what they wanted. After Phi had been gone for a year, I received a letter from him in which he told me the truth about what he was doing. He said he did not have enough food to eat and worked very hard. I paid for a boat trip to Ca Mau, walked two hours into the jungle and found him. He was so skinny I hardly recognized him. I gave him money to buy food so he could survive. It broke my heart to see my beloved brother so mistreated. He was finally able to return to Bac Liêu the following year.

The only thing I could do was work for the Communists, as did the rest of my family. So in 1977 I was hired to work at a store operated solely by the Communist government. This store was comparable to a giant Wal-Mart. We sold clothing, material, gasoline, food (mostly rice), and various other goods. Everyone had to buy whatever they needed from this store. Families were required to shop only at specific times of the year. The Communists sent each family a letter telling them when they could shop and how much they could buy. This required people to stock up on items for many months at a time. I was paid a small salary, about twenty-five cents per hour, but my family was able to buy items at a discounted price. The government owned everything and tightly controlled it all. Limiting how much gasoline a family could have severely curtailed how far people could travel away from home. Most people no longer could afford to drive their car or motorcycle. Vietnamese people lived at the mercy of the government in all aspects of their lives. We worked everyday. There was no such thing as "weekends." Only those who worked directly for the Communist government were fortunate to be granted a couple of days off from time to time.

While working at the store I lived at a friend's house nearby. The store was part way between town and my parent's home in the jungle, about four miles from Bac Liêu. I was fortunate that I was able to see my family and grandparents regularly. One day a small group of Communist soldiers came to the house. With them were twelve people they had caught trying to escape the country. Leaving Vietnam was illegal at that time. The soldiers knew I worked for the government, so I was considered a "friendly." They wanted me to search the female prisoners before they were taken to jail. I knew one of the women. She was eighty-five, and her son operated a cigarette store in Bac Liêu. I took the woman into a back room on the pretense to search her, knowing there was no way I could do that to her. She cried and asked me if I would get a message to her son, letting him know what had happened to her. I reassured her I would. Then I asked if she was hiding anything in her clothing and she told me no. That was extent of my search. When we came out of the room, the soldiers accused me of accepting a bribe from the old lady and not searching her as I had been instructed. "I did not take her jewelry, and I did search her," I reassured them. They kept after me, insisting I had not done my job properly. Finally the soldiers believed me and left with the prisoners. My heart was pounding in my ears. I was so relieved when they left.

Later that evening my friend and I went to the Bac Liêu jail and gave food to those twelve prisoners. Most of them were people like me, whose only crime was to search for a better life than this one under the Communist rule. Our boss at the store did not know we provided food to the prisoners, or else we would have lost our jobs. One night, after visiting with the prisoners, I was overcome with sorrow for them. I went home, unable to quit thinking about these people, not knowing what would befall them.

I do not know how I found the courage, but I crept back late in the night, to help them escape. The local jail was not a closely guarded place. It seemed that the fear and terror instilled into us civilians by the atrocities we had lived through were sufficient to ensure our cooperation, even when held as prisoners. So when the careless guard on duty fell asleep, it was easy enough to take the key off the hook that hung outside of the jail, unlock the cell door, and free all twelve prisoners.

The next day the soldiers realized the prisoners had escaped and a search was immediately initiated. The only prisoner who was caught deserved it because he was so stupid. The soldiers were searching on motorcycles they had taken from local citizens, and this one escaped prisoner saw a soldier riding around town on the motorcycle that had been taken from him before he had been arrested. That man became so mad that he began yelling at the soldier to give him back his motorcycle, saying it was his property and the soldier had no right to be riding it. The soldier recognized the man and arrested him, taking him back to the jail on "his" motorcycle.

It was not unusual for soldiers and smugglers to extort money from people trying to leave Vietnam. Smugglers would make arrangements with the people who wanted to leave the country, quote a high price for their passage, take their money, and tell them to meet at the designated boat that night. Then the smugglers would tell the soldiers about the prearranged meeting and get a reward. So instead of meeting the smugglers, the desperate people would encounter soldiers and be arrested. Many people were kept in jail for nearly a year before being released. They lost their money, their freedom and their hope. From 1976 until 1978 many people left Vietnam secretly, risking their freedom and their lives in search of a better country. Many successfully left after bribing officials, yet many died or were jailed.

I was determined that one day it would be me leaving this dreadful country. As a child, I could not envision myself ever leaving Vietnam or ever living without war raging. But now as a young woman, I knew I would die before staying here for the rest of my life. Vietnam was no longer my country.

9

I continued working for the Communists throughout 1977 without any other major incidents. In early 1978 I had moved from my friend's house to the store where I worked. Some of my friends already lived there, so I decided I would too and be close to them and my job. The previous year I had begun to seriously think about leaving Vietnam. I knew I needed to pursue a better life than the one I had. My life would always depend upon the Communists, and I knew they would never let me or my family rise any higher in status or acquire anymore material things than what we already had. Life for them was as good as it was ever going to be but it was not good enough for me.

The incident that finally led me to that difficult decision happened in the latter part of 1977. One day before going to work I had heard that the Communists had arrested several people who had arrived in Bac Liêu from Ho Chi Minh City intending to leave Vietnam. Being near the ocean, Bac Liêu and Ca Mau were the two easiest exit points from the country. There was always boat traffic in and out of our area because fishing was still a big industry. Boats, big and small, were a primary mode of travel for this part of the country. The Communists would stand at the docks and write down people's names and the purpose of their trips as they boarded the boats. The standard reason everyone gave for getting on a boat was "fishing." If the people noted on the lists did not return as anticipated, then the Communists would arrest and jail their family members. It was never a pleasant experience.

The Ho Chi Minh City people who had been arrested were brought to my store by the soldiers. All their belongings had been taken from them, which included two bags of gold one of them had brought. The soldiers had placed their suitcases, backpacks, and sacks into the back room. When I arrived at work later that day, I noticed all of my coworkers were wearing the clothes and jewelry that had been confiscated from these people. I was sickened by the sight. Those people had hopes and dreams of a free life, and now silly girls who had been brainwashed by the Communists were parading around in their clothes, flashing the jewelry that had been passed down for generations.

I learned that most of the people who had been arrested had paid smugglers $1,500 per person to be taken out of Vietnam on boats. The smugglers had arranged to meet them at a certain spot during the previous night and then had alerted the Communists of the meeting. There was no one that could be trusted during this time. The next day two of my friends and I went to see the prisoners at the jail and took them barbequed pork, mangos, and cigarettes. I always had a soft spot for prisoners after having my father and brother arrested during the war years. I knew how hard it was on the prisoners as well as their loved ones.

Some weeks later a Chinese man, Hon, came to the store to see a friend of his who worked with me. Hon lived in Ho Chi Minh City but had come to visit his parents in Bac Liêu. Hon and I became fast friends, never romantically involved, but simply friends who could talk to one another. We were both twenty-one and had our whole life in front of us. But the life we were living was a hopeless one and we knew it. We refused to settle for it like our parents.

Eventually Hon told me that he planned to leave Vietnam like so many others. The Chinese people hated the Communists as much as we South Vietnamese did, and all wanted out of Vietnam. Hon's uncle owned a boat, and Hon planned on leaving the country on it. One day Hon invited me to leave with him. His uncle was rich enough to afford a pilot for his boat who had the reputation for being the best around. "This pilot can take us through any storm," Hon reassured me. Hon's family had made a lot of money from their plastics factory in the former Saigon and from the crops they grew on a large amount of land they owned.

We decided we would leave together the following Saturday. Hon was going to send a friend of his on his motorcycle to pick me up at my friend's home at 8 p.m. About an hour before I expected his friend to arrive, I went to retrieve the backpack I had packed a week earlier and hidden inside my friend Ha's bedroom closet. Ha did not know I had placed the bag in her house because I was afraid the Communists would arrest Ha and her family if they suspected she had helped me. Her house was next door to a coffee shop where the soldiers liked to meet in the evenings and catch up on the day's events. When I got to her house, I noticed several people milling about and talking and laughing. I knew if I was seen coming out of a house carrying a backpack, it would raise suspicions. "What should I do?" I fretted to myself. I decided I would walk to Hon's home without my belongings and without waiting for his friend to arrive.

As I approached his house I noticed storm clouds hanging low over the ocean. It had been raining all day and it did not appear to be slacking up at all. I hid behind some tall ferns where I could see Hon sitting on his porch. I just sat there on a rock, wanting to run to Hon, yet too scared to leave my hiding place. "What," I wondered, "would become of us in a boat if the storm continued tomorrow?" I was terrified of drowning in the ocean. I saw Hon get up when his friend on the motorcycle appeared. Hon's face dropped when he saw I was not on the bike. An animated conversation broke out between the two men, and Hon sat heavily back on the porch. He put his hands over his face and then I realized he was crying. Hon and I had never exchanged words of love, and in fact I did not love him, but I knew he could save me from a wretched life.

I finally left and returned to my room in the store. The next day the sun was shining gloriously; it was perfect sailing weather. I learned that Hon had left in his uncle's boat and that his parents had thrown a fit when he had told them he wanted to wait on me. They would not allow him to remain in Vietnam one more minute for a fickle girl. The Communist soldiers had followed Hon to his boat that night and threatened to arrest him, but Hon's parents gave the soldiers twenty gold bricks to let him leave. Would they have given any gold bricks for me if I had been there? I doubt it.

Hon's boat carried eighty-five other people to freedom. It should have been eighty-six, but I had been too scared to chance it. I never talked to Hon again. I heard he settled in Australia, where years later I sent him a letter. But he never responded. In all likelihood, he was probably still mad at me because I had delayed him long enough for the soldiers to learn of his escape plan, causing his family to part with their precious gold.

A few days later I saw a boat return to the Bac Liêu dock. It had set sail about ten days earlier but had gotten lost in the storm and had to return. Word quickly spread through town that during the storm a little four-year old girl had suffocated to death because there were so many people packed together. This incident confirmed my fear of boats and the ocean. But I still knew in my heart that I had leave Vietnam. There were few jobs available, and children were not able to attend school if their parents did not have the money to pay for it. Most children from ages four to twelve were forced to help their families earn money by selling food in the streets, making maybe a dollar a day, and that was a good day's wage. I knew it was not the life for me.

After Hon had left Vietnam to a world unknown, I became very sad. "How could I have been so stupid, so fearful, and not go," I chastised myself. I realized just how much I had liked Hon, or was it just the idea of escape I liked? As the months dragged on I became more resolved to leave this place. If I did not, I knew that my life was meaningless, like so many others who just settled for being told what, when and how to do everything. I had bigger dreams than that.

A few months after Hon's departure, my brother Phi married; then a couple of months after that my sister Thùy married as well. I was the only who had no ties to this land anymore. "I will leave," I said to myself over and over as I lay awake at night. "They cannot keep me. I will be stronger and face my fears." But could I really do it? My own thoughts mocked me. I questioned my resolve when I was helping in the kitchen and Grandmother cut open the shark-half she had purchased at the market. A human foot fell out of the shark's body.

I did not know if I could really face the ocean's dangers and flee this place after all.

10

In 1979 Thùy's mother-in-law, Vinh, told me that some of her family members were going to leave the country and I was invited to join them. Vinh said her family was going to depart from Ca Mau, and we would go there to meet them. I readily agreed. I was overjoyed that the opportunity had finally arrived and that I would be leaving with family. Buddha was smiling on me, I thought. If I only had known of what was to come I would have run back into the jungle and hid.

Now, in 1979, for that one year only, the Communists had opened up the opportunity for people to leave Vietnam more easily than any other year since the war ended. The Communists had instituted a plan called the "Orderly Departure Program," which ended the illegal "boat people" exodus from the country. All one had to do was to pay the Communists a one thousand dollar departure fee. They allowed anyone to leave who could pay. This meant that most poor people had to remain in their dreary surroundings, making the best of their circumstances.

I was in a compromised position. I worked for the Communists, and I knew that when I put in my request to leave, the soldiers would ask me, "You do not love your country? Why would you want to leave?" The day came and I prepared myself for the questions. "Oh yes, sir, I love Vietnam and the government. They have been good to me and my family. But I am the only one in the family who is not married or has small children. They depend on me to help with expenses. So if I can work temporarily somewhere else, I will send the money back to them, here in Vietnam, and they can spend it on the government items." They accepted my answers that felt so transparent and gave me permission to leave.

I did not tell my parents that I was leaving. I made Thùy promise to keep my secret so I would not run the risk of Father and Mother talking me out of my plans. They could find out after I had left.

I remember the day clearly. On May 2, 1979, Vinh took me to Ca Mau to meet her son Bao, her daughter Nhan, Nhan's husband Hung, and their four children. All of them were going to leave the country and would look after me. I felt safe to be with a group of family, not my blood family, but my sister's family, a close enough kinship for a refugee!

Upon arriving in Ca Mau, I discovered I did not have enough money for the passage fee. I met with the boat's owner and explained my predicament. Since I was a good cook, I offered to work for my passage. He agreed and hired me to be one of the shore cooks for the passengers while we awaited the day of departure. However as we were striking the deal, the owner's niece joined us and saw my hands. I was wearing two rings my mother had bought me years earlier, one jade and gold and the other a simple gold band. I treasured those rings because my mother gave them to me, and they were the only things I owned with the exception of a few clothes. The owner's niece demanded I give her uncle the rings for my fee in addition to my new cooking duties. I did. I sacrificed them in order to get out of Vietnam. Little did I know at the time this was only the beginning of my sacrifices.

Because of bad weather our departure was delayed for four days. Finally the day arrived, the day I had been waiting on for years. My first steps toward freedom were beginning, and I was so excited. The boat was large; approximately twenty-five yards long and five yards wide. There was a small enclosure on the upper deck that contained the steering wheel and other instruments the captain needed to operate the boat. The remainder of the deck was flat without side rails, which I thought looked dangerous in the event a large wave washed over the boat throwing anyone who stood on the into the sea.

The wooden boat was brightly painted blue with a red stripe running along the top. The front hull had an eye decorating it along with the boat's registration number, BL0773. There was a stairway that led down into the boat's lower deck. This lower deck ran the length of the boat and contained one of the two engines. The majority of the 540 people were placed into this area. There were no windows or means of fresh air for those who traveled in the lower deck.

The day we left a Communist soldier met us at the dock and wrote down each of the passengers' names as they boarded. As I was getting on, the soldier told me the boat was not large enough for that many people and predicted I would die in the ocean. He then said, "I should arrest you, and at least you will be alive." I was terrified. Why was he targeting me and no one else? I had received permission from the government and had paid for my passage. What else could they want from me? "Leave me alone," I thought to myself as he talked to me; "I have come this far, and for once I will face my fears." I steeled myself, and just looked at him, giving him the opportunity to do whatever he wanted. He eventually tired of his mental game with me and motioned for me to move on and get into the boat. I relaxed and, with weak knees, climbed aboard.

Only the "important" people were allowed to sit on the top level. When I got on board, I saw Nhan and her family on the top level sitting in the enclosure since Hung was a nurse. I immediately sat next to them and refused to move when I was told to go to the lower level. There was no way I would be placed where I could not see and smell fresh air. Bao, my sister's brother-in-law, was made to go down to the lower level since the captain would let only about twenty-five people remain up on top. The thought of being crushed in with more than five hundred people made me shudder. I thanked Buddha for letting me remain where I was.

We left Ca Mau at three o'clock in the afternoon of May 6, 1979. It was my passageway to a new life. The excitement and fear we all felt was palpable. As the boat drifted further out into the ocean, I felt myself becoming queasy. I had heard about people getting seasick and was grateful I had the foresight to buy a small plastic bag to take with me in case I too became sick. "Great," I thought, "now, I have to throw up in front of everyone." I quickly realized I was not the only one who was seasick. I swallowed my pride and decided I better make use of my bag instead of just sitting there! That night, while moaning and groaning and holding onto my stomach, I also had to endure listening to one of the female passengers hollering through a bullhorn. Her job was to keep the sailors awake throughout the night. I was not going to get any sleep either I realized.

I felt much better the next day, finally getting my sea-legs. I had started the trip with six oranges; however, when I woke up I discovered they were all gone, taken by the other people while I slept. The wind increased that second day, causing the waves to swell. As the day went on, the waves grew larger and larger, until eventually the boat rocked violently, as if we were on a roller coaster. After thirty minutes of violent movement, the wind suddenly stopped, and the water was calm. Then the rains came down in a torrent; all the while the sun was shining through it. It was the most peculiar storm I had ever seen. Finally the weather cleared, and we dried out.

Eventually, the boat entered the waters of Thailand. But we were careful of the Thais, fearing they would rob us. We had heard stories of pirates plundering the boats of other refugees. My friend Muôi and her husband had left Vietnam a few months earlier. I learned that their boat had been attacked by pirates. Muôi's husband was killed and thrown into the water, so Muôi jumped in after her husband's body and drowned.

As the day approached sunset, we saw another boat off in the distance headed in our direction. We grew apprehensive. These pirates knew that the people in boats such as ours had left their homes and country with all their precious belongings, including money and family heirlooms, mainly jewelry. The pirates knew we were defenseless and took full advantage of the easy pickings.

We watched the boat get closer and closer, not sure what to do. Maybe it was a friendly boat and not the vicious thieves we feared. As it got nearer I recognized it as a dreaded Thai boat because of the large lettering on the side of the boat. I called out, "It is a Thai pirate boat!" One woman sitting near me yelled at me. "Be quiet! You do not know what you are talking about. If you say it is a pirate's ship you will bring all of us bad luck! Do not say another word." I insisted that I recognized the letters being Thai even though I did not know their meaning.

They approached us slowly and then circled our boat four times. The boat contained the captain, a Chinese man, and eight others. It was similar in design to our boat, even painted blue and red, but it was smaller, only about two-thirds the size of ours. We were scared into silence. What did they want? Would they kill us after they robbed us? We knew there was no one who would help us. We were truly alone in the middle of the South China Sea.

The boat finally stopped a distance away from us, facing us. No one spoke a word. The only sound was the noise of the water lapping at the side of our boat. What were they going to do? It was eerie, watching them watch us. Suddenly, the Thai engine revved up, and the boat started toward us, its speed increasing as it made its way directly into our side. Too late we realized what was happening and our captain was unable to react quickly enough. The Thai boat rammed us hard, causing Hung, Nhan's husband, to fall overboard. Several men reached over and pulled him back into the boat.

A hole was ripped into the lower level of the boat. Many told me later that those down there were soon standing in water chest high, so they began stuffing blankets, clothing, anything they could find, into the hole to stymie the water flow. I could hear them screaming. They had not been able to see the Thai boat coming at us and did not know we had just been attacked by pirates. After we had been rammed, I immediately left the enclosure and sat out on the deck. I was afraid if the boat sank, I would be trapped inside and drown.

The Chinese captain pulled his boat alongside ours, and his men boarded us. They carried knives, threatening us. We were terrified. They started taking our jewelry and money. They walked among us, roughly pulling rings, necklaces and earrings off people. I had a pair of gold earrings my mother had given me, and I was determined to keep them. One woman was standing near me with her little boy. I asked her if I could hold the boy, telling her it would calm me down. She gave him to me, and I held him securely in my arms. I thought the men would leave me alone if I held a child.

As the pirates walked among us, I hid the earrings in the hem of my shirt. When they approached me, I placed my hands to my ears and throat, indicating I did not have any jewelry. One of the Thai men (actually more of a boy, probably only seventeen or eighteen) acknowledged my cooperation, thanking me for being good. Bah, I was not being good; I was being a survivor, as I had been all of my life. I returned the boy to his mother after the men had moved past me.

It is amazing to think back to the incident and realize how docile we were. We numbered over five hundred, and they were only seven, but they dominated us. We Vietnamese gave up too easily. We had grown tired of fighting and knew the horrors of killing. We did not want anymore of that life. The Thai were able to subdue us because we let them.

After the pirates got what they wanted from us, they jumped back into their boat. It was then that I became afraid their captain was going to capsize our boat. No witnesses meant no consequences. I felt desperation rise in my throat. I did not want to drown out here where no one would ever know what had happened to me. No, I decided right then, I would not be docile any longer.

As the boats drew level next to each other, I instinctively jumped onto the Thai boat. I do not know how I found the courage to do that. Another young woman (she was about nineteen and was with her family) followed my lead and jumped after me. But she mis-timed the motion of the two boats, which were bobbing in the water in opposite rhythms. Her leg was immediately caught and crushed between the boats. She shrieked and fell into the Thai boat. I looked over the side and saw sharks circling in the area where her broken leg had bled. The Thai captain must have had a change of heart perhaps because he realized our boat would sink soon due to the hole he had made in its side. He instructed about fifty people to get onto his boat, leaving the 490 others to remain on our boat.

Once I was on the Thai boat, two of the sailors grabbed me by the arm and pulled me toward the captain's quarters. I struggled with them, crying and begging them to leave me alone. One man roughly pushed me, saying, "The captain will be pleased with you.

You should be able to make him more pleasant to be around. Do as you are told and we will not hurt you. The captain is not mean; you could do a lot worse than this man." I knew what they meant. I had been chosen to be used by the captain for his pleasure.

I started praying to Phât Bā Quan Âm, considered to be an angel in the Buddhist religion. As I prayed to the blessed figure, the captain harshly called out to the sailor who held me, telling him to leave me alone. He had no interest in a young Vietnamese refugee who was unkempt and poor. The men pushed me back down on the deck and told me to stay put.

The captain threw a tow rope to the Vietnamese boat. He said he could not take us to Thailand because he and his men would get into trouble for piracy. However, he agreed to tow us to Malaysia. He then handed out blankets and food for us. Obviously, he had a capacity for feeling bad about what he had done to us.

At about five a.m. the next day, when we were still about two hours from the Malaysian coast, the Thai captain announced he was not able to enter those waters while towing us. He gave our captain directions to Malaysia, so I and the fifty others returned to our disabled boat. The rope tying the two boats together was severed.

Our boat was sitting much lower due to the water it had taken on; however, the items that had been pushed into the hole had slowed the flow. The captain told us that we would be okay since land was not too far away, but that we had to throw everything we owned overboard to reduce the weight. This included throwing away our food and water. We had to choose either to drink and eat while sinking or replenish our supplies in a few hours when we reached the coast. It seemed to be an easy decision at the time. Only we had no idea what we would face once we did find land. We still held out hope that a better life awaited us in a few hours.

11

That morning stretched out, and the boat bobbed up and down incessantly. Water continued to slowly flood the lower level. People in the lower level had to stand in the sea water as they waited for land to appear. I could hear them crying and demanding to be told what had happened. Those of us on the top deck called out to them, reassuring them everything would be all right. The young woman whose leg had been crushed between the boats moaned and cried out in pain. Her cries were difficult to listen to especially since there was nothing any of us could do to ease her suffering. She drifted in and out of awareness, and the rest of us were grateful when she lapsed into unconsciousness finally silent. Each of us became quiet as well, lost in our own thoughts, wondering if life or death awaited us.

Eventually we saw land on the horizon. As our boat drew closer to the shore, we saw numerous coconut trees and clean white sand, but no people. However, as we got closer, we were able to discern houses up on the beach nestled among the trees. We were so relieved to get to land. Nothing could be as bad as the last two hours, wondering if the Thai captain had given us the correct directions or if the boat would sink before arriving. Here we were though, and I felt all would be well.

Upon landing on the beach we were met by Malaysian soldiers. We immediately let out a cheer upon seeing people, believing food and shelter were close at hand. Several people jumped off the boat, anxious to get on shore. As they did, the soldiers began violently hitting them with whips made out of stingray tails. Those tails were sharp at the ends and drew blood. The soldiers began yelling for the people to get back on the boat and stay there. After everyone scrambled back on board, the soldiers stepped away, back towards the shore. We sat there stunned into silence. Now what? Did no one want us? As we waited without a sound, a wail went up, making us turn around and look. The mother of the injured young woman had her hands covering her face and was rocking back and forth. Her daughter had died in her arms. Yesterday she was a nineteen-year old woman who had her whole life ahead of her, and today she was dead.

A man sitting to my left instructed me, "Start crying so the soldiers will let us off the boat. They will feel sorry for us if women are crying." So I did, and amazingly it worked. Others joined me and we cried and begged for help. We told the soldiers about the young woman who had died from blood loss. We were allowed off the boat but were made to sit in the beautiful but very hot sand. The soldiers had us place the dead girl's body on a piece of wood and push it out into the ocean. We stood there watching it slowly drift out to sea until it disappeared. Her parents' cries of sorrow still haunt me.

The Malaysians did not give us any water or food. We were told to sit on the beach under the burning sun where we stayed for several hours. As we sat there, the soldiers came around to each of us and wrote down our names and addresses as well as the names of our family members. I grew worried. If I gave my correct information, I was afraid the authorities would arrest my family in Vietnam and take away their property. I might be prevented from ever seeing any of them again if I was arrested and not allowed to return to Vietnam. I quickly decided I would not reveal my true identity. It was just too risky. When the soldiers approached me, I told them my name was Mỹ Phuong Tran, which was my paternal grandmother's name, and misrepresented my date of birth by adding on a few months. I told them I was alone and did not have any family with me or back in Vietnam. It was because of this lie that my family still cannot visit me in America. There is no official record that a "Mỹ Phuong Tran" has family in Vietnam or that my family has a sister or daughter in

America named "Tuyet Anh Phạm," which is my birth name. Little did I know this was the first of several new names I would have.

Several hours later we were finally given canned fish to eat but no water. One lady had some rice (from where I had no idea) which she cooked there on the beach. It smelled so good that my mouth started watering. She gave some to Nhan, Hung and their children, but Hung angrily told her not to give me any since I had not helped cut the wood for the fire. "No, take back her bowl, she has not earned it," he demanded. "What did you do to help?" he sneered. "Did you find the wood, fetch the water from the sea, or do anything?" He yelled at me until his face was red. Everyone just sat there without saying a word; all of them seemed to have been stunned into silence. The intensity of his anger made my heart pound. I was holding a bowl of the rice in my hands when he said these things, but I dropped it and walked away. I stayed far away from my sister's family after that. Years later I heard this family settled in Canada. It is still very difficult for me to think how cruel Hung was to me that day. I thought of us as family and was shocked at how quickly he had turned against me and no one stood up for me. I felt abandoned.

I walked amongst the people on the beach, devastated by the selfishness I had just experienced. I eventually sat with two single sisters, and the three of us looked after each other. Meanwhile Nhan and Hung were arguing bitterly, their fragile emotions frayed. Hung hit Nhan in the head causing her to bleed. They were fighting because their children cried for water. Bao, Nhan's brother, came over to where I had settled and asked if he could stay with me. He said he had to get away from the fighting. I told him, "No, you cannot. You did not take up for me, and I will not take care of you. Neither you nor your family can be trusted." He turned away from me and rejoined his sister and her children.

Days went by, and we were confined to the beach. We had no shelter from neither the blazing sun nor the pouring rain, although we would creep toward the meager covering from the coconut tree branches. The soldiers had placed barbed wire around the beach, cutting us refugees off from the nearby town. We were treated like cattle. The soldiers would pass out small cans of food such as potted meats and sardines. We were never given water. We had to cook with water from the ocean, making the food nearly inedible due to the saltiness. We drank rain water whenever we could catch it. One Malaysian woman called out to me through the fence and offered me food in exchange for my earrings. I declined the trade desperately wanting to hold on to those mementos from my mother. There were 539 of us crowded into a small area, and we stank. Our bodies were dirty and sticky from the salt water. The soldiers would not give us soap to clean ourselves.

One night a soldier saw me curled underneath a tree when yet another rain storm came. He took pity on me and gave me a piece of heavy plastic to shelter myself from the rain. I was grateful but also scared that he would expect favors from me. It was common at night for the soldiers to take young girls and women away from the crowd and rape them. Girls who were fortunate had blankets and often hid under them so that the soldiers would not see and take them. I was fortunate not to have been attacked as so many others were.

In the mornings soldiers walked among us, swinging the stingray whips, randomly hitting people and yelling, "Jump into the ocean and bathe yourselves. Run and do not come out until you are clean. I can not stand to be around you because you stink." Thankfully I avoided the whip while many others fell victim to it. We all would run into the water, knowing it was futile since the salt water never cleaned us. We suspected it was just a way for the soldiers to exercise power over us and belittle us. I quickly learned if I told them I was sick the soldiers would leave me alone. They would not hit me or make me get in the water. I look back on it now and realize I was more fortunate than many others. I was not raped, was given covering, and escaped the whip.

Day after day went by without a word of what we were waiting on. Why would the Malaysians not let us leave the beach? "Why not give us a boat and let us leave if they do not want us in their country?" we wondered. Finally three weeks after landing on shore, we were told the Malaysian government had decided it would not accept us, and we had to leave their country. The soldiers then told everyone to put their jewelry in a basket they passed around. We were robbed once more. Again I successfully hid my earrings in the hem of my shirt. After collecting our jewelry, the soldiers gave each of us a mat to sleep on and lined us up in single file. Four smaller boats were brought to us, our new escape vehicles. All of these boats had engines but only one was furnished gasoline. The other boats were supplied to us without fuel. The fortunate ones who got on the fueled boat were the wealthy refugees, the doctors, a general, a nurse, anyone who still had money and jewels to offer the Malaysians. Needless to say I was not on that boat. These four boats were to carry 540 people, no . . . I mean 539 since the poor girl had died.

Of that number, 147 got into my boat, a small wooden fishing boat that was approximately twenty feet by ten feet, built for only about twenty to thirty people at most. We could only sit up straight in the boat since there was no room to lie down or stretch our legs. The boat contained a small enclosure built for protection from the blistering sun or pouring rain. This enclosure was painted blue and red, colors often displayed by fishermen for good luck. Only about ten people could be inside it at any given time, even though it was originally built for the captain and one or two of his crew. Just outside of the enclosure was a hole in the floor that opened into a section underneath the main area of the boat where the fish were stored until the fishermen returned to land.

As we were preparing to leave, Nhan came up to me. I had not spoken to her since that first night on the beach three weeks earlier when her husband would not allow me to eat rice. She offered me a seat on their boat since I was family. Her boat was the one with the fuel supply. I declined her offer, quickly turned away and got into another one of the boats. I had nothing left to say to her.

The Malaysian navy towed the four boats out to sea with the promise we were being taken to Indonesia. We looked forward to finally being taken somewhere we would be treated with respect. We had no idea that once again we had been told lies.

We were towed all through the night. The next morning the sailors cut the tow lines. We started yelling, asking what was happening, why were they doing this? Many people began crying, begging for water since we had not been given any rations or supplies. As our boats began drifting away, the sailors told us to follow the sun and we would find land soon. Then they started shooting guns in the water, and we quickly grew quiet. The Navy boat sped away from us. How were we to follow the sun? We had no motor, no paddles, we were adrift. After about four hours I could no longer see the other three boats. We sat in silence, bobbing up and down in the ocean, no land or people in sight.

A few people had some cans of food they had saved from our stay on the beach; but not me. I had given my cans away to people that I thought needed them more than I. I had never dreamed I would be sent out upon the ocean again; otherwise, I probably would have been wiser about my rations. I was worried about what I would eat and drink. As the others ate their food and discarded the cans, I picked them up and drank the leftover juice from the food. I did not know a soul, and no one cared about my welfare. Was there really a god watching over me? I had never felt such intense loneliness. There was no one to help me, no one who cared if I lived or died. I missed my family terribly and wanted only to return home. Maybe Vietnam was not so bad after all, I thought. At least I had food and water and could be with my family regularly.

One woman somehow had secreted a small bottle of water onto the boat. I believe she had brought it with her from Vietnam and had held onto it through our stay in Malaysia. One night I saw a man steal this woman's water. The next day the other men realized what he had done and began calling him evil and threatening to throw him overboard. He begged for mercy, explaining how thirsty he had become while bailing the ocean water out of the boat. It took too much energy to continue arguing with him, so the other men eventually left him alone.

In an effort to show kindness amidst all the ugliness, I gave a woman my hat so she could catch rain water. She caught some during a brief rain shower and then refused to give me any. It seemed all of the people had become so cruel and insensitive in their attempt to survive. I knew that was not the type of person I wanted to become. Did 'survival of the fittest' mean one had to lose her humanity?

One day a Chinese man named Danh grabbed a fistful of seaweed as it floated by and began eating it. No one else followed his lead, probably knowing the salt content could kill a person. Danh was about a year older than I. Poor Danh, although he survived the seaweed diet, I remember that once we were settled in Norway, he was beaten severely at a Christmas gathering when he sang a Communist song because it was the only song he knew. His teeth were knocked out, his left arm was broken, and his face swelled so much that he was hardly recognizable. Maybe some people are just barbaric in time of stress, like on the boat, and maybe others are born that way regardless of the circumstances.

12

While we were adrift we took turns climbing in the water to clean ourselves. We held on to the side of the boat and let the water flow over us. Even though the water was salty it felt refreshing to wash away the sweat and body fluids. It also gave us a moment to relieve ourselves with a sense of privacy.

During our fourth day at sea, a Philippine military ship came near us. It was large, flat ship that looked like it was built for airplanes to take off and land. I could see the sailors standing on the deck in their uniforms. We frantically waved and shouted at them, but they either did not see us or chose to ignore our pleas for help. We yelled repeatedly for drinking water, for a tow to safety, for food, for mercy, all to no avail. The boat eventually moved away from us with our cries apparently landing on deaf ears. The devastation we felt was overwhelming. How would we survive without food or fresh water? We had no way of propelling or steering the boat. We could float in this vast sea forever and never be found. I had lost nearly all hope; even so, I still kept praying to Buddha while others prayed to some deity named Jesus. Our spirits were at their lowest.

The days passed by slowly while the sun mercilessly beat down on us. Some of the people would climb into the fish hold in the boat's bottom in order to escape the sun's heat. The ones who had originally sought shelter in the enclosed area would not give up their place in the shade.

The ocean struck relentlessly against the sides of the boat. I thought the noise was going to drive me over the brink into madness. Slap, slap, slap, all day and all night. The only thing we could think of was food, food, and more food. I took on the role of encourager, talking about various foods, the tastes, the smells, the spices, just so the saliva flowed in each of us. "The soup is boiling on the stove and the smells of potatoes, carrots, cabbage, and pork float in the air. There is shrimp cooking with the special *nuoc mam* sauce poured over it. For dessert, we will eat our fill of fried noodle covered in coconut milk and sugar," I described our meal in great detail. Our mouths were so dried out that we could barely swallow. My banter seemed to cheer up the other passengers, and they kept asking me to continue with my culinary descriptions.

Everyone else's canned food was gone after the sixth day. As for me, I had had no food from the first day we were placed on this motorless boat. All I had consumed was sea water and the little bit of fluid left in the discarded cans of fish. The sea water made me even thirstier, but I had no choice but to drink it or risk dehydration. Suddenly, the diarrhea hit me. My insides felt twisted inside, and the cramps were unbearable. I was miserable. Even in this setting I still had my pride. The last thing I had to hang on to was my dignity, and diarrhea threatened to take even that from me. Whenever I felt the urge coming on, I jumped into the water and relieved myself. It was all any of us could do. No one ever seemed to notice me. All acted as if they were in a trance.

The days were hot and humid, draining our remaining strength. On the sixth day, the rain we had been praying for arrived. The storm was strong and accompanied by blustery winds and high waves. It seemed that everyone became seasick. Since our boat did not have a motor, we had no way of steering across the waves. We were at the mercy of the sea. At times the boat almost capsized, throwing us from one side to the other. I immediately started to pray to Buddha to save us when suddenly the waves calmed down and the boat righted. The rain and wind immediately went away. It seemed to be a miracle.

Even though we were thankful for the refreshing rain we had nothing in which to catch it. All we could do was to open our mouths and let the sweet water fall onto our tongues. One lady had a panel from a parachute that her family had gotten from an American soldier during the war in Vietnam. She had hauled this parachute panel from home to Malaysia to this boat drifting aimlessly in the middle of the South China Sea. She successfully caught some of the rainwater from the passing storm in the chute. Later that night I asked her for a drink, I was so thirsty, and she gave me one mouthful of blessedly salt-free water. At sunrise, when there was light, I saw what was in the chute and immediately got sick. The water was black and putrid. The chute had been slept on for the three weeks we were on the Malaysian beach, and who knows where it had been before that. I now know God made me ask for the water during the night when I could not see how bad it looked. He was saving me from death by dehydration, even if the rescue was nasty.

There was a Chinese family of five on the boat with me. The three children were probably age three and younger. Once the storm abated the parents began screaming at each other, threatening to kill one another. The woman was blaming her husband for getting her into this predicament and told him how much she hated him. I began crying, begging them to stop. They ignored me for a while, consumed by their own emotions. The woman then began threatening to throw her oldest child overboard, a three-year old daughter, because she no longer had the energy to care for the girl. The woman then turned on her other two children who were cowering down and screamed that she would throw them into the water as well. The father just looked beaten down and did not say a word. He had no energy to fight for his own children.

I spoke up and told the woman that I would take the oldest child and care for her during the rest of our journey. The parents looked relieved at that suggestion, and the woman gladly handed the girl over to me. The woman seemed to calm down, and she stopped her threats to throw the other children overboard. The whole incident was alarming in that no one else on the boat spoke up except me. I believe that if I had not offered to care for the girl, she would have been tossed to the sea, and 146 other people would have just watched her sink beneath the surface. I held the child close, and she clasped her arms around me. We comforted each other as best we could.

Once the storm had moved away and the sky cleared, the men found a long stick lying in the fish hold in the bottom of the boat. They took turns using the stick to push us through the water. It seemed pointless since the stick was not in the shape of paddle but rather much like a long broom handle. It was difficult to get any water pushed past us at a reasonable speed. One man yelled for everyone to reach over the side and paddle with their hands. I was so short I could not reach the water no matter how hard I strained.

After a short while the man who was taking his turn at paddling placed the stick into the water to give it another pull. When he did, the stick hit something hard. He cautiously tapped the stick up and down trying to determine what object he had hit. We watched him thinking we had run into a sandbar. Yet it would have been very odd to find a sandbar way out here in the middle of the deep ocean. We all stretched out our necks trying to get a glimpse of the unidentified object. I saw it with my own eyes, but I still can not believe it. I just knew my mind had turned to mush due to the heat. But I swear to this day, the hard object appeared to be a whale underneath our small boat.

The whale, or whatever miracle it was, carried us on his back for the next two days. I knew I was living in the midst of a miracle. All 147 of us were praying for some type of divine intervention to make the whale take us to safety rather than pull us further out to sea to eat us. Even though it was a marvelous entity, we did not know if the whale was going to be our helper or our destroyer. None of us had any previous experience with whales! Was what I saw during this time a hallucination? A miracle? Both? I am convinced this was some extraordinary creature that had come to my small boat.

The nights on the boat were so cold. The water would periodically spray me in the face, making me shiver. It was difficult to get any sleep or rest. I began to understand why the little girl's mother had gone mad. No sleep, no food, no water, and three small children to worry about would drive anyone crazy. All of our clothes had become dirty and torn due to the salt water and sun damage. The fabric ripped whenever we moved around. We all looked bedraggled, homeless, and exhausted. The days and nights had grown monotonous. The girl and I clung to one another, periodically peering over the side of the boat to catch a glimpse of our whale. We still could not believe what was happening.

On the eighth night of our journey, we saw lights in the distance. We had no idea what the lights were but desperately hoped they meant we were close to land and civilization. We could make out three distinct areas of lights in the east, west and north. Our hopes soared. We all began to believe the whale was carrying us toward safety. The days continued to go by, and each night we saw the lights still shining, beckoning us, drawing our mysterious savior ever closer.

The eleventh day dawned. My mind and body had deteriorated without any food and only a limited amount of water for nearly two weeks. My senses and thoughts were sluggish. I dozed as the day droned on with the whale still carrying us to parts unknown. As I slept, I had a dream about a battle between good and evil. Both entities were pulling on the people in my boat. A divine tug of war raged as I later learned had been foretold in the Bible.

I awoke from the dream and realized the boat was moving much faster, more so than in the past several days. As we all watched, the boat closed in on the objects that had held the lights we had seen the last three nights. Oil derricks had lit up the night sky. The water was slapping the sides of the boat hard. It seemed the whale knew he was close to the destination where he was to drop off his passengers. All of us strained to see any signs of human life on the nearest derrick.

At around noon that day, the whale finally completed his divine duty and took us directly to the middle derrick. It was a Canadian one. There were numerous small lights encircling the steel structure, making it look as if it had been decorated for Christmas, a holiday of which I had no knowledge at that time. We looked up into the soaring formation and saw several men wearing orange life vests looking down at us. We guided our boat close to a nearby steel girder and tied the boat to it.

One of the workers called down to us but quickly realized he did not speak our language. He hollered out to the other men, and eventually one man stepped forward who was able to speak a little bit of Vietnamese. He told us that we could not come aboard the derrick but would have to remain in our little boat. He explained that about a week earlier another boat, similar to ours had arrived and the people in that boat had been allowed onto the derrick. However they had been too distracting to the production responsibilities of the workers, so they could not afford a second disruption. Those first arrivals had been taken away by a helicopter a few days earlier.

We cried and pleaded with them to allow us to get out of our boat but to no avail. Remaining on our small boat was becoming difficult both physically and mentally. We felt trapped and claustrophobic. We had not been able to stretch our legs unless we jumped into the water. The oil workers dropped containers of blessedly fresh water down to us which we greedily consumed. I drank three bowls, much to my regret later. We told them we also needed food, and the men sent down spaghetti and meatballs for the adults and Granny Smith apples for the children. We had never seen spaghetti and did not know what it was. We thought it was a different kind of rice, but ate it anyway. My stomach became bloated, and I was sick for three days. I had not eaten any food or had any substantial quantity of water in twelve days and my body could not absorb what I had devoured.

After we had made contact with the oil workers we realized the whale had left us. He had parked our boat in a safe place and left us, his job completed. The workers told us that a huge storm was headed in our direction and would arrive in about two days. At that moment, about two hundred white fish began jumping out of the water all around our boat. I believed it was another divine sign that we would be taken care of and for me not to worry about the impending storm.

The oil workers assured us that they had contacted a military ship from Norway to come pick us up. We stayed tied to the derrick for three days, all the while the workers keeping us supplied with food and water. The first night our rope broke, and the boat began drifting out to sea away from the derrick. The Canadians heard our cries and hurried to throw us another rope we used to secure us once again.

Finally the third day brought the Norwegians to our rescue. Their ship was huge, resembling a cruise ship. We had to crane our necks to look up at it. The ship could not get too close or else our boat would be swamped. They circled around the derrick and lined up until it was in a position to back up toward us, ever so slowly. I later learned that this was the first time that Norway had assisted any refugees from war-torn Vietnam. It was June 15, 1979; I was twenty-two and felt much older.

The ship's crew began helping all 147 of us off the boat. The Norwegian sailors were a welcomed sight to us. They were clad in their white sailor hats, white short-sleeved shirts, and black pants. I felt safe in their presence. As I walked toward the rope ladder, my legs buckled underneath me. I was too weak to walk. I was still taking care of the little girl and was unable to carry her, so I handed her to a sailor. I then just lay in the bottom of the boat, the last one on board, scared I would be left behind. But one sailor climbed down and picked me up. He carried me to another sailor who passed me on up the ladder. Once I was on the ship, I suddenly realized I had left on the small boat my backpack which contained the few pieces of clothing I had managed to keep. But it was too late to retrieve it. The sailors had sunk the boat so another ship would not mistake it as having passengers and waste time and resources to check it out.

Once I was on the Norwegian ship, the little girl returned to her mother. I guess the mother decided that now they were safe she really did love her daughter. She never thanked me for helping nor did she ask if she could help me. I kept on learning just how selfish people can be in desperate times.

Later that day the predicted storm approached us. The waves grew as tall as a three story building. The Norwegian captain informed us that this was much larger than just a storm; it was a hurricane, and it would be in full force by tomorrow. The ship left at full speed in order to get out of the hurricane's path.

The sailors gave me some milk and food when I first boarded the ship to help with my weak legs. Then I was given two big towels and shown where to shower. A shower was such an unbelievably wonderful experience. My hair was heavy with dirt, salt, and oil. I stood under the spray of the warm, clean water, savoring the feel of it as it cascaded over my body. My joy at being clean can not be described. It was simply magnificent. I wore the two towels I had been given because my clothes were dirty and stinky, and too ragged to put back on. I had tried to wash them as best I could in the shower, but they needed to dry out before I could wear them again. Once out of the shower, all I could manage was to lie down on the deck feeling blissfully safe.

My first real meal consisted of a boiled egg, steamed cabbage, mashed potatoes, and rice. I felt rejuvenated. Boiled eggs and cabbage never tasted so good! I then found an isolated corner on the ship, lay down on the towels, and took a much needed nap.

Twenty-four hours later we finally landed in Singapore having traveled 367 miles. Our little boat would have been devoured by the waves, and if it had not been, there was no way we would have been able to drift that far to safety without either starving to death, dying of dehydration, going mad, or all three. "Divine intervention is interesting," I thought.

I have never told anyone about the jumping fish, the whale, or the way the people acted toward each other, because I did not think I would be believed. It is still surreal to me like a bad dream, the kind of dream from which you cannot wake up. Those two weeks were another lifetime ago. If I had been told while I was still in Vietnam that I would have to endure these experiences, I do not think I would have ever left my country. I surprised even myself that I could survive the ocean.

Singapore was beautiful. Everyone seemed happy and some of the people I had traveled with thought of it as heaven. Of course any place that was not the ocean seemed heavenly to me.

13

Upon our arrival in Singapore we were taken to a building where we were individually interviewed. I was asked the names and addresses of my family. As in Malaysia, I feared that if I gave my true identity, my parents, siblings, and grandparents risked retaliation for my leaving Vietnam and not appreciating all the "good" things the Communists proclaimed they did. Anyway, I had never liked my birth name, Hồng Anh Phạm. Tuyet means "snow" and Anh is often used for a man, a masculine identification I disliked. So I decided to keep the name Mỹ Phuong Tran that I used in Malaysia. Phuong is a word for a brilliant red flower that grows on a tree, while "Tran" is my grandmother's maiden name.

I could not remember my true date of birth. I knew I had been born in the Year of the Rooster, which was 1957, but most Vietnamese never celebrate birthdays, since we mark our birthday from the day of conception and not the actual day we arrive in this world. *Rich* Vietnamese celebrate their birthdays because they think everyone cares about them! The rest of us only celebrate the milestone years, such as turning fifty. So I told the Singapore interviewer that I had been born on November 6, 1957, making up that date on the spot. I have since learned I was really born on February 15, 1957, by the Chinese calendar, which is the month of March by the calendar used in the United States. I know—it is all very confusing. My family has never known I changed my identity that day in Singapore. If my loved ones were to tell the Vietnamese government they were leaving the country to visit Tuyet Anh Pham (my birth name) or Mỹ Phuong Tran (now my new name) in the

United States, there is no record that either of these persons ever left Vietnam to live in the U.S.

After the formal interview and proper documentation were completed, we were placed on a bus and taken to a dirty apartment complex about twenty minutes outside of the city. The building consisted of one long room and had no partitions or doors separating men from women. We all slept side by side. Luckily I secured a spot next to the window so I could have fresh air. Unluckily though, insects came through that window along with the fresh air. One morning I woke up to find a caterpillar crawling on my neck. It was huge and hairy. I jumped up screaming and clawing at the vile thing. For all the horrible events I had been through, one would think I could stand something to touch me that would eventually turn into a lovely butterfly!

As part of the refugee amenities that Singapore gave us, we received two dollars a day to spend on whatever we wanted. One of the men who had survived the ocean ordeal with me and who was also from Bac Lieu, was hired by the Singapore government to hand out clothing and other items to us since he spoke our language. One morning I was sent to the clothing room by one of the workers and saw the man sorting the clothes. As I began looking through the selection of clothing, he grabbed me, trying to hug and kiss me. I struggled against him with all my might and began yelling as loud as I could. I broke away from him, threw the clothes on the floor, and ran back to the main room. I refused to accept any clothes offered by the assistance office after that.

Several days after arriving and settling in, I ventured out into Singapore by myself, walked around for a while, and finally sat on a bench in front of a large building. I noticed a Chinese man walk by with a group of his friends. He saw me sitting alone and came over. He introduced himself, Binh Tong, and he was so handsome. He looked about two years older than I. Even though I am half Chinese from my mother's side of the family, I did not speak his language and he did not speak Vietnamese. Fortunately one of the men in his group had been on my boat and spoke both Chinese and Vietnamese, so he interpreted for us. Binh told me that he wanted to give me food and clothes and would come back the next day. Binh lived and worked at a construction site in Singapore and seemed as if he truly wanted to help us refugees. The next day, Binh arrived as promised and gave me clothes, food and other small items. We saw each other regularly after that second meeting.

One day, deciding to go further into the town and explore more of the area with some of my fellow refugees, I rode the bus. I had dressed in what I thought was one the prettiest dresses I had been given. During the trip a man on the bus asked me why I was wearing that particular outfit. "I am not sure you realize it," he said, looking uncomfortable, "but, do you know you are dressed in a nightgown?" I was dumbstruck and refused to get off the bus once we arrived in town.

In August, about two months after arriving in Singapore, the refugee office told me that I was going to be sent to live in Norway. Of all the places in the world, I did not want to go there because I had heard it snowed there and was very cold. Plus there were hardly any other Vietnamese living in Norway. But I had no choice in the matter. I was at the mercy of other people and other countries, so I did as I was told by the officials. The day before I was to leave, I underwent a medical check-up. I guess the Norwegians wanted only healthy people in their country.

My departure day came just twenty-seven days after I had arrived in Singapore. I felt sad because Binh and I had developed a friendship, not a romantic one, but he was nice and had a gentle way about him. I had been so lonely since leaving Vietnam, and having a friend was important to me. Binh had talked about helping me remain in Singapore so I could be close to him. But first he would have to buy me a passport, and the only place he could do that was in Malaysia. A passport would cost about five thousand dollars, and he just did not have that much money. I understood since I did not have any money other than the daily two dollar allowance from the Singapore government. Sadly, we both realized there was no way I could stay.

Binh met me at the bus station where I would catch a bus to the airport for the trip to Norway. He gave me a watch, a clock, and 675

Norwegian Kroner (the currency), which is equal to one hundred-thirty-eight U.S. dollars for my trip. As we said goodbye Binh began to cry, which made me cry. We still had a language barrier, but we clearly knew each other's feelings.

When Binh left the station, the bus was still not scheduled to leave. As I sat there, I decided I would stay in Singapore after all. Norway just did not seem to be the right place for me. I left the station and walked into the city. I walked for hours wondering "What is to become of me? Where will I live? How will I make money and pay my way? Who will I have to talk with?" Perhaps I would find Binh.

As time passed I grew more worried. I imagined living on the streets of Singapore and being taken advantage of or worse, raped and killed. Eventually I saw a bus that was empty and climbed on it. I sat there for about an hour before the bus filled up with other passengers. Finally it made its way back to the station from where I had started. The other refugees with whom I had traveled so far were still waiting. Along with several other Vietnamese who had arrived independently from us, sixty-five of us from my little drifting boat were flown to Norway,

14

We landed in Oslo, Norway in August 1979, after spending thirty hours on the plane. Some of the refugees got off, but I remained on because Oslo was not my destination. After another five or six hours in the air, I finally arrived at my new home, Khristainsand, Norway. There were sixty-seven of us left. We had come so far, leaving a warm climate, as well as our families. But we had similar dreams: to live in a country that was not ruled by the Communists and to have the opportunity of a better life, both materially and emotionally.

For some reason the Norwegians immediately began calling me by the name "Nina." I guess they could not pronounce Vietnamese names. Luckily for me I had arrived in Norway during the warmest time of the year, even though by my standards it was still very cold. I was used to hot and humid weather, not these near-freezing temperatures and snow on the ground. "They call this 'warm?'" I wondered shivering.

We climbed aboard a bus and were driven through the small town to a two story building on the outskirts. An older lady in her mid-fifties greeted us. Her face was red from the cold air, yet she was pretty and pleasant. She showed us where we would sleep. I was placed upstairs with another single Vietnamese lady to share a bedroom and bathroom. A basket on each of our beds contained various toiletries such as shampoo, soap, deodorant, and other small necessities. I was grateful to have these items, for I fully appreciated being clean after my stay on the beach and journey in the boat during my exodus from Vietnam. Most of my life I had bathed in salt water, so now I thought I was living in luxury having fresh water at my disposal.

My roommate was called "Helen" by the Norwegians. I never knew her Vietnamese name. Helen, who was thirty-two, was ten years older than I. In addition, I quickly learned that she was an unpleasant woman, treating me and everyone else dreadfully. Helen would throw away my food and take other items of mine without asking. After just a short while of rooming with Helen, in order to get away from her I moved to another part of the building, a cold glassed-in porch. To find some warmth at night, I would sneak inside the building to sleep on a table in the living room. After a month of this miserable existence I was given the room formerly occupied by a family who had moved out.

When I initially arrived in Khristainsand, I had no socks, shoes or coat, but that did not keep me from walking around the town. I walked through the snow, crying the whole time because of the cold. The snow came up to my mid-thigh. I was used to sweltering heat and humidity, not this white stuff! Finally Debbie, one of the refugee workers, saw my plight and gave me a scarf, gloves, and a coat. My feet were also taken care of once I bought myself some proper foot wear.

Through an interpreter I asked Debbie how I could get to the United States. America was my ultimate goal, not Norway. She told me that since I had been rescued by a Norwegian military ship, I would have to stay here. I was discouraged, for I could not imagine living the rest of my life in this freezing world.

About a month after arriving in Norway I accompanied fifteen others from my building on a grocery shopping trip. We yearned to eat rice, our main staple that we had not had in many months. Upon arriving at the store we realized it was closed and would not open for an hour and a half. All of us sat down in the snow and patiently waited. Finally the store opened and I bought a box of rice. I cooked it that evening and it was the best rice I had ever eaten!

In our building we shared one kitchen with a stove and a refrigerator, cooking our own meals with the food we purchased with our $300 the Norwegian government gave us each month. This $300 was placed on a credit card, and we were expected to buy our food and clothing with it. We took turns cooking on the single stove since we did not share our food with each other. We had learned during the war and while being adrift at sea that we had to fend for ourselves. This mindset kept us from sharing and made us suspicious of each other. We hoarded our food and trusted no one. This way of thinking was reinforced when I discovered the other residents would take whatever food they could find in the refrigerator, often leaving me without my meal.

By contrast, Debbie helped me a lot; she was a mentor to me. Once she took me to her home and let me spend the night. It was like sleeping in heaven, a real home and a cozy bed, prizes I was determined never to take for granted. Another helpful person at the refugee building was a Spanish nurse. A few weeks after I had arrived she showed me a magazine with a picture of a man named Elvis Presley. He had recently died, and all of the United States was in mourning. "The king is dead," declared the headline. "I did not know the United States had a king," I said. The nurse patiently explained to me who Elvis was and that the pills he had taken had killed him.

My first Christmas outside of Vietnam arrived. Being a Buddhist I had never celebrated Christmas and did not know the significance of the day. In Vietnam we called the holiday "Noel" but did not celebrate the birth of Jesus as did the Catholics. It was a holiday all Vietnamese celebrated with gift-giving and festivals, but Buddhists did not place the Christian emphasis on it. Once the war ended and the Communists took over the country, Christmas celebrations became more private, especially for the Catholics.

A party was arranged for us refugees at the local Christian church in Khristainsand to celebrate the season, and I planned to dress in my finest outfit. I had a friend make a red dress and a white pair of pants for me from fabric I had purchased, and in return I cut her hair. I thought I looked very nice. I arrived at the party and marveled at the decorated tree, which was the first one I had ever seen. The Norwegians sang Christmas songs, even though none of us understood the words. Still it was beautiful music.

I was not quite so stylish at another social gathering. I was invited to attend a dinner at the church, and I knew I needed to look my best. I fixed my hair in a fashionable style, put on a new outfit and arrived eager to eat and socialize. As I entered the room, I noticed a woman approaching me. Thinking she was going to assist me in finding a seat, I smiled at her. She did not return the smile. "Oh no," I thought, "she does not seem to be glad to see me. I wonder what I have done wrong." She glared at me and said, "Nina, you need to go back to your room and remove the two big pink curlers from your hair and take off that nightgown! Put on clothes that are more suitable for church." Why did I seem to have such trouble identifying pajamas? I was mortified yet again.

The clothes I bought with the government assistance never seemed to fit me. The pants were always too long. I assume the clothes were made that way because it seemed that all Norwegians were tall and were not made with short Vietnamese people in mind.

Two families volunteered to help me learn their culture and language. Each one took turns meeting with me and trying to teach me simple words and phrases. They, as well as all the people I met in Khristainsand, were very nice to me. They loved to give out hugs and chocolate.

Despite these kindnesses, in February 1980, I began to get very depressed. I had begun to feel trapped in Norway and helpless about not being able to get to the United States. It seemed there was nothing to be thankful for in my life. I had left my family thousands of miles behind me eight months earlier, had changed my identity so no one could ever find me, could not speak the local language—I felt so lost. One night I took a bottle of pills from the nurse's station, not knowing exactly what they were, and ran to my room, locking the door behind me. I took five of the pills just like Elvis, and drank some shampoo, unlike Elvis. What was I thinking—shampoo?

The nurse realized that I had taken the bottle and tried to get into my room to see what I was doing. When she discovered the door was locked, she yelled for help. No one could get the door opened, and I did not respond to their shouts. She called for an ambulance and when the emergency medical workers arrived, they kicked in the door. When I did not respond to them, the medical workers pinched the skin on my neck. I was told later they did that in order to rouse me from unconsciousness, which it did. The pinch was so hard that it ripped my skin. I promptly woke up and shouted at them to stop.

They took me to the hospital and put tubes down my nose and throat, cleaning out the mess I had ingested. During my stay there, an Australian lady named Sally, who worked for the government in Khristainsand, came to visit me. She was very nice and helped me when I was discharged. Upon my release I was taken to live in a dormitory of a college that was about a day's drive from the city. Apparently, they believed a change of scenery would be good for me.

I lived alone in a room on the second floor. During the day I attended classes along with the college students, but since I could not speak Norwegian, I sat there not comprehending anything. I did not want to learn their language because my heart was set on living in the United States where English is spoken. After class I would walk around exploring the campus. The girls who lived in the room next to mine often invited me to get together with them at night, which was a lot of fun. Among them was another Vietnamese lady who was able to translate for us. The girls would quiz me on my life and ask me all kinds of questions, such as what Vietnam was like, how I survived the war, if any of my family had been killed in the war, and how did I get all the way to Norway by myself with no money. They were very friendly and tried their best to cheer me up. They laughed at how fast I talked, which is normal for Vietnamese, telling me I made them tired just listening to me.

Around 11 o'clock at night, I would return to my room then cry myself to sleep feeling homesick for my family and desperate to start a new life. I felt so alone even with these nice girls trying to be my friends.

There was one girl with whom I began to feel comfortable. She drank milk in such a way it left her with a moustache, which she had no idea she had. She walked around all day with dried milk outlining her upper lip. I would laugh at her, and of course she never really understood what I found so funny until one day I showed her. We both laughed at her surprised look. After about two months I returned to Khristainsand, leaving the college with mixed feelings. I was ready to leave but also knew I would miss my new Norwegian friends.

Upon my return the Vietnamese man who assisted the refugee workers by translating our language to English and French told me that I could not go to America because I did not have any money. He said, "You need to work and save your money so you can afford to travel to France. Once you get there, you will be in a better position to get approval from the French government to continue on to the United States. The Norwegian government is not going to help you get there."

But I was not going anywhere else, I had decided. It was America, the land of the free, where I wanted to live—to make my country. I did not want to make France my home. I kept asking anyone who would listen to help me achieve my goal. It finally worked. A few weeks later the Vietnamese man and Sally's husband took me by train to Oslo. There I met with the workers at the U.S. Embassy to see what could be done for me. I was told I would have to stay in Norway for a year. Additionally, before I would be allowed to travel to the United States, I would have to show the authorities I had family already there.

While she was in Oslo Sally had contacted the local newspaper and asked them to run a story about me. The story told how I had no family in Norway and that I was desperate to go to America. The story explained that in order to get there, I would need a family to adopt and sponsor me. We returned to Khristainsand and waited for a family to contact me.

The next month I received some good news. A family by the name of Nu had indicated they would adopt me. The Nus had emigrated from Vietnam and settled in Oslo in 1975. They had six sons who ranged in age from twelve to twenty-six. I eagerly waited for their eldest son to travel to Khristainsand to take me to my new home in Oslo. As the days went by I became more and more anxious.

My former roommate, Helen, had heard about my unsuccessful suicide attempt and how that gesture had opened the door to my adoption. I guess Helen thought the same thing would work for her. She drank a large bottle of whiskey, became sick and passed out. But poor Helen, her scheme backfired because the only new home and family she got was the mental hospital. Everyone in our boarding house was glad she was removed because she had been so mean and strange, such as the time she flooded the house by leaving the faucet on for hours and another time she chased me through the house threatening me with a knife. Helen was allowed occasional visits out of the hospital, and each time, she asked me to help her. I felt sad for her and would cry, but I knew there was not anything I could do for her.

Finally, in March 1980, the day came. My new "brother" arrived and took me "home" to Oslo, Norway. The Nus lived on the third floor of an apartment building. I could open the window in my room and look down on a green lawn outlined by beautiful landscaping. Cranberry bushes lined the sidewalk to their building and I would grab a handful of berries as I walked by and gobble them down. It did not take too long before those bushes became bare.

At first, the Nus were nice to me. After I had moved to their home, I found out they were from North Vietnam. Traditionally South Vietnamese, such as I, do not trust a person from the North. I had seen how the North people had taken over the businesses and homes of my friends and neighbors in Bac Liêu, and I believed they could not be trusted. However, I was determined to make this work. I was willing to do whatever was necessary to get to America. Mr. Nu was a welder and Mrs. Nu was a housewife. I quickly discovered I had been brought there to clean their house and cook their meals. "I can do that," I thought, "if it helps me get to America faster."

Part of the agreement I had with the Nus was to pay them $200 per month for rent. I did not have any money or an income and was not sure how I would do this. Once I began living with them, my monthly government assistance check of $300 was to be sent

112

directly to the Nus since they had become my caretakers, so I had only the $100 left over for myself.

Fortunately for me, a Norwegian man named Noah, who was a friend of the Nus, had heard about my plight and wanted to help me. Noah contacted me and said he would pay the $200 a month rent so I could save all my money for my trip to America. Noah's brother worked at the U.S. Embassy, and Noah agreed to intercede on my behalf. Noah was a good man, about fifty-five years old, and so kind. He did not expect anything in return other than that I would realize my dream one day. I truly believed that my life was finally on the right path.

Shortly after my arrival Mr. Nu talked his boss into hiring me to clean the cafeteria located in the shop so I could earn some extra money. I needed all the money I could make to pay for my trip to the United States. Every day for two weeks I went to the business after lunch and cleaned. Mr. Nu and I walked home together talking about our day, the people at work and a variety of topics. It was a pleasant time. I enjoyed having a father-daughter relationship with him. However, Mrs. Nu was not so happy for me.

It soon became apparent that Mrs. Nu felt some animosity toward me. Whatever her reasons, she began mistreating me. She complained incessantly that my cooking and cleaning were substandard and that I was not paying them enough money to stay at their home. Eventually, I had all I could take from that woman and decided to leave.

In May 1980, after three months of living with the Nus, I searched out Noah. I had no one else to turn to for help. Noah sent me to live with some Catholic sisters at a nearby hotel. I was given my own room, and the sisters cleaned my room for me as if I was a special guest. They were so nice to me. Finally I felt some peace of mind.

A cross and a crucifix hung in every room at the hotel. I really did not know what these items symbolized and could not understand the sisters' explanation. One day I saw several people walking to a Catholic church that was near the hotel and decided to follow them. I had always wondered what went on inside a church, other than the dinners and parties I had attended. I knew what happened in a Buddhist temple, but not in a church.

Fortunately for me on that particular day the service was being conducted in Vietnamese. I finally heard about Jesus and felt a stirring in my heart. After the service I approached the Father and told him I wanted to be baptized. He said "Nina, you need to learn more about Jesus first because it is a big decision," and he gave me a small Bible written in Vietnamese. The priest took the time to explain Christianity to me and encouraged me to read the Bible before committing my life to God. I kept attending the services over the next several weeks, learning more and more, but not enough to get baptized.

During my six weeks with the sisters my life was quiet and contented. I would walk around town during the day seeing the sights. At night we ate a delicious brown cheese and bread. One day, during my regular exploration of the city, I met a group of American students. They tried to communicate with me. I was fascinated by their American clothes and the confident way they carried themselves. They gave me their names and addresses and encouraged me to call them once I arrived in the United States. I was so excited about my visit with them and thought I would have friends once I arrived in my new country. During my remaining travels I lost the paper that had all their information on it and was never able to contact any of them.

Even though my life was serene, I still wanted to be an American. Workers at the U.S. Embassy had told me that if I had family in the United States, I would be approved to live there. I realized that unless I did something about that requirement, I would never get there. I had to take matters into my own hands and not continue waiting for everyone else to take care of me. I had come too far and endured too many hardships and lonely nights to give up now.

I knew of a family friend from Bac Liêu, Toan Ngo, who had settled in Amarillo, Texas—wherever that was! After much searching with the assistance of the staff at the Embassy I found his address. I wrote to him and asked him to pretend to be my uncle and write back to me. I waited and waited, anxiously looking for a response each day. Finally the letter arrived. I gave it to Noah, who gave it to his brother at the Embassy. After a few more worried days, I was told the government had bought me an airplane ticket to the United States of America, my new home. I was so excited that it seemed my heart would jump out of my chest. My dream was coming true. I would be an American soon, very soon.

15

It was August 1980 when I received my airline ticket to the U.S. However, before leaving Norway I was required to undergo another physical examination. I guess they wanted to be sure I did not have any disease that would infect Americans. As it turned out, my lung x-ray was not clear, so a second one was scheduled a week later. I was extremely disappointed at the delay then fear replaced my disappointment. Was something wrong with me; maybe a disease from all those weeks drinking sea water and not eating; or maybe walking through all that snow without proper clothing weakened me. I feared the worst.

I began praying to Jesus like I had learned at the Catholic Church. I read my Bible and tried my best to understand it, knowing God would help me. He just had to; that was what gods did for their devoted followers. About an hour after receiving the bad news about the x-ray, an Embassy worker called to say a second x-ray would not be necessary after all. I had been cleared to fly to the United States. Another miracle had just happened in my life. I continued to be blessed.

I went to the Embassy in Oslo and was given a letter to carry with me. The letter was written in English and explained who I was, where I was going, and that I could not speak English. This letter was to help me during my travel whenever I needed assistance, either catching my connecting flights or finding a place to eat or the restroom. I made ten copies of it to hand out during my trip.

A helpful Embassy worker took me to the airport and dropped me off at the front entrance. Here I was, a small woman from Bac

Liêu, South Vietnam, on my way to a new country full of people with whom I could not communicate, yet with whom I would make my home. As I sat in the waiting area I heard voices over the loud speaker system. Of course I had no idea what they were saying, so I just sat waiting patiently. A man, another passenger, finally approached me and said, "Excuse me ma'am, I think they are calling your name." His hand motions conveyed more than his words. The airline gate attendants were looking at me and waving their arms. I jumped up and ran to the boarding area. Once in my seat, I began showing my letter to the other passengers. When we landed in Denmark they were nice and helped me find my connecting flight.

Since the flight from Denmark to the United States was not full, I had plenty of room to stretch out. Exhausted, I lay across the seats in my row and fell asleep. The flight attendant came by and woke me up saying I could not use all the seats since I had a ticket for only one. I curled up in my seat trying to get comfortable, and drifted back to sleep, so deeply that I missed the food and drinks that were handed out later in the flight.

Then I arrived in Chicago, Illinois, the United States of America. The South China Sea, Malaysia, Singapore, Norway, even Vietnam, seemed like a lifetime ago. I had to catch another flight from Chicago to Amarillo, but once I entered into the Chicago airport terminal, I realized all my fellow passengers from Denmark had left me. I found myself alone again.

I saw a police officer standing in the terminal and tried to ask him for help. Searching my pockets for a copy of my precious letter I discovered I did not have any more copies. I had given all them out on my flight from Denmark. The officer took me to the police station, perhaps thinking I was an illegal alien since I had no identification, only my airline ticket. The officer called the number on the ticket and verified that it was legitimate and I was lawfully in the United States, even though I am not sure who told him that. Then he took me back to the airport. Unfortunately my flight had already left. My luggage had been on the airplane, so I was left without extra clothing or overnight necessities. However, the airline staff was able to place me on a later flight that same day.

At Dallas, Texas, I was required to change planes for the final leg of my journey. I was learning that flying was tiresome. Being a passenger was exhausting whether I was on a plane or a boat. When I entered the airport terminal in Dallas I looked around in amazement. People were wearing cowboy hats and boots, just like they did on television. All I knew about Texans was what I had seen on television, which I had always believed was reality. "These people are cowboys who are on their way to kill Indians," I thought. I was more than a little intimidated. I knew how to handle Communists but was at a complete loss on handling cowboys or Indians.

Hours went by as I sat in the boarding area—a copy of all the others from airport to airport, country to country—until finally, an airline employee approached me. She was Vietnamese and explained I had missed my flight from Dallas to Amarillo, Texas, and there would not be another one until tomorrow. This nice lady took me to a fancy hotel near the airport for the night. My luggage was in Amarillo while I was stuck in Dallas. A man who had missed his flight like me and had to stay over, heard the employee explaining my predicament to the hotel clerk. This man tried to reassure me the hotel was safe and that he would watch out for me. He patted my arm and smiled.

My room was luxurious, with a queen-sized bed and a large bathroom. The other hotel guest, the man who had spoken kindly to me at the front desk, was in the room across the hall. He made motions that I interpreted to mean I was safe and to sleep well. However I was afraid he was a bad man and only wanted to take advantage of me. "Why else is he being so nice to me? That is how the Viet Cong act, nice yet deadly," I thought. When I did not see a manual lock on the door, I feared he would try to get in my room during the night.

To test how secure my room was, I left the room and closed the door behind me, quickly discovering I could not open it. I stood in the hallway for a minute trying to figure out what I should do. The only thing I knew to do was to go to the man's room across the hall and ask for help. I tentatively knocked on his door and he answered, wrapped in a towel, fresh out of the shower. I tried to tell him about my dilemma using simple sign language. He just smiled and gestured for me to wait. He went back inside and dressed then took me downstairs to the front desk where he was able to get another key for me. I realized how wrong I had been about him. He was very nice, and I did sleep deeply.

I was up early the next morning to continue on to my final destination, Amarillo, Texas. It was August 14, 1980. I was met at the airport by my friend, Toan Ngo, who had pretended to be my uncle and written the letter to the Embassy while I was in Norway. He was accompanied by his three brothers. They had agreed to let me stay at their house.

Amarillo was so different from Bac Liêu. The city was full of cars without any bicycle traffic. There were no open-air markets and I missed the sounds and smells of the ones back home. But I liked the cleanliness of the city. All the streets were paved and toilets were inside the buildings! I could finally have some privacy.

The local Catholic Church sponsored me because they were involved in assisting Vietnamese refugees settle in the local area. Church members tried to help me find my own place since my stay with the Ngos was to be only temporary. They first wanted me to live with a sixty-year old lady who needed help with basic housekeeping and other chores. I was scared to live with someone with whom I could not communicate; however, I decided to give it a try. After my first night with her, using hand signals and body language, she indicated she wanted me to make her breakfast. She also wanted me to stay at home with her because she was lonely. I felt uncomfortable with the arrangement, not knowing her and unsure what to do all day, so I called the parish Father and told him I had changed my mind and asked if he would take me back to my friends' home. A few days later a second family came to meet me to see if I would like to live with them. Since they had a son who was close to my age I did not think it was proper for me live in the same house. So again I declined a nice offer and remained with Toan.

I noticed my relationship with Toan and his brothers began to deteriorate. One of his brothers did not like me. I never understood why, but he became increasingly spiteful toward me. Maybe he was jealous of my adventures or I did not respond to him in a way he wanted. He accused me of saying bad things about his family. I am not sure who he thought I talked to since he and his family were about the only people in Amarillo that I knew. He would raise his voice at me and then attempt to get his brothers to side with him. Eventually everyone in Toan's family began to treat me differently, like I was a burden. They rarely talked to me and when they did, it was with impatience and resentment. I decided I had to move into my own apartment. I began making plans, knowing it would take some time to find work and save enough money to move.

Khan, another brother of Toan, had a brother-in-law, Sanh Van Tran, who lived about forty minutes north of Amarillo in a small town called Dumas. Even though we had the same last name, Tran, we were not related. Sanh came to Amarillo on weekends to visit his family and share a few beers. His brother-in-law helped him get a job at a local beef packing plant, so Sanh moved to Amarillo permanently. He was very quiet and spoke only when someone spoke to him. Sanh appeared comfortable just listening to conversations rather than being involved in them. However, we noticed each other right away. I caught him glancing at me several times but he quickly looked away whenever our eyes met.

To my surprise I learned he had been the pilot of Hon's boat. Hon was the young man in Bac Lieu who had first asked me to leave the country with him. I had backed out at the last moment because I was scared of the stormy weather. Sanh had been hired by Hon's uncle to take Hon and the others away from Vietnam. I quickly learned the American saying, "It's a small world."

A Vietnamese couple who had been in the United States for about five years, assisted me in securing a job in the cafeteria at the same beef packing plant where Sanh worked. I was paid $3.35 an hour, bringing home $89 each week. I saved every dime for a month and was finally able to rent my own apartment. Since I did not know how to drive, I paid people $5 a week to take me back and forth to work.

A month or two after I had arrived in Amarillo, I had my first experience with an American festival called a "fair." Three of my friends I had met at work took me to the Tri-State Fair. There were rides, food, and various craft displays. There were even pens of animals like goats, cows, and sheep were kept. Other than the bright lights and cotton candy, it reminded me of the market in Bac Liêu.

As I walked around, trying to take in all the exhibits, I realized I had become separated from my friends. Panic quickly rose in my chest. I walked all over the fairgrounds but could not ask for help since I still did not speak English. I started to cry, suddenly remembering when my mother took me into the jungle and Father would not let me return to my grandparents' home in town. I was all alone again. I finally went outside the gates to the parking lot, and there were my friends, standing around wondering what had become of me. They quickly surrounded me realizing how upset I was. I did not lose sight of them again that night.

Sanh quickly became a regular visitor at my apartment. Our courtship was not typical of those in Texas. We rarely spoke and never shared our adventures we had lived through during our journey to Amarillo. We simply looked at each other and shyly remained quiet. Our first conversation consisted of me finally getting the nerve to ask him if he wanted any watermelon, which to my relief, he did.

Sanh did not ask me to marry him. It was as if we had an unspoken agreement that we would be with each other. In October 1980, four months after meeting, we married. Our marriage was without any legal arrangement but was instead a private exchange between the two of us promising we would stay together forever. On November 4, 1981, one month before the birth of our first child, we decided to become formally married by the laws of the United States, so we went to the Justice of the Peace. However, before he would agree to marry us, he had to be satisfied we were not related to one another since both of our last names was Tran. He told us that if we were relatives we could not get married. We convinced him Tran was a common name in Vietnam and that we were not related. After several assurances, the judge finally agreed to perform the ceremony.

We exchanged wedding vows in English. Neither of us had any idea what we were saying but obeyed when the judge said, "Just say

'I do.'" So we did! Sanh gave me a wedding ring that cost $25. The judge wished us luck and told us he did not want to see us come back later asking for a divorce. Afterward, we held a party at our apartment for our friends to celebrate our special day.

The judge had given Sanh a can of shaving cream and me a bottle of liquid soap as wedding gifts. Unfortunately I did not know the soap was for dishes, so I used it to wash my hair. A few weeks later I saw a commercial on television with a woman using the same soap, Dawn, to wash her dishes. I felt so stupid and then worried for days that my hair was going to fall out. One of my friends reassured me nothing like that would happen. I was so embarrassed.

In the summer of 1983, we renewed our vows in the Catholic Church just to be sure the marriage had been properly blessed by God. I guess a triple exchange of promises to spend our lives together sealed us as one.

Epilogue

During my first year of living in Amarillo, I was visited by an associate pastor of the First Baptist Church, a Korean whose mission was to personally contact Asian persons who had newly immigrated to Amarillo. I let him talk me into attending the Baptist church, where I realized how much God had done in my life and that He had a divine purpose for saving me through all the trials I had experienced. I decided Buddha was no longer the god for me. I gave my heart to Jesus Christ finally knowing exactly what that meant and was baptized. Sanh held onto his Buddhist beliefs and would not have a thing to do with my Christian God. Many of the Vietnamese who lived in Amarillo were Catholic. Because of my language barrier with the Baptist pastor, I decided to go to the Catholic Church where a large number of Vietnamese people attended. The priest spoke my language and he began meeting with me individually to teach me about his religion. I quickly embraced his beliefs.

After Sanh and I were married I began learning English with the aid of a nun sent to me by my priest. More than anything I wanted to become a United States citizen. The nun came to my apartment every day for about an hour, patiently teaching me the difficult language. She gave me a Vietnamese-English dictionary that was invaluable in translating my world into the American world.

My time with the priest gave me the opportunity to learn about the Virgin Mary. He invited me to join his church, which I did. I felt so welcomed there and knew in my heart that this was where God meant for me to be. "How would I have ever known about Amarillo, Texas, and all the wonderful opportunities that awaited me, if I had remained in Bac Liêu?" I thought. I may have been a scared young woman, but I was determined to have a better life than my family whom I had left behind. God was my leader now, not the Communists.

For eleven years Sanh and I lived in the same one bedroom apartment. We had our three children during that time. I became pregnant with Carolyn, my first-born and only daughter, while I was working at the beef packing plant cafeteria. I was fired a month before she was born. The reason the plant manager gave me was that my pregnancy prevented me from carrying the heavy loads of dishes. However I knew that was a lie. By then I had learned enough English to understand my boss when she had been talking to the plant manager and told him I had left my work area without permission. I was a good worker, a hard worker. I had never avoided my duty and always given my best to the job. In fact, this job was easy compared to the fishing operation I helped with in the jungles of Vietnam. I knew I had done nothing wrong. It was my first experience with injustice in America, and it hurt my feelings.

I had no insurance to pay for my baby's birth once I lost my job. Sanh had not worked at the plant long enough to have insurance either, so we had to find $700 quickly to pay for the doctor and hospital costs. Fortunately the doctor agreed to let me pay it out at fifty dollars a month. A few days after I was fired, I was at my apartment looking at the front window. I saw my former boss in the parking lot. She was there visiting a friend and was unaware I lived in the same complex. When I saw her, my face became hot with rage. I guess I was like my father when it came to my temper.

Although she was a big lady, much taller than I, I confronted her. I have no idea where I had picked up the stick, but there it was, in my hand. An older North Vietnamese lady was outside watching all the commotion and yelling at me to hit the other woman. I shouted at my former boss, declaring her to be the meanest person on earth, a heartless woman. That is when she pushed me. Being nearly nine months pregnant, I just toppled over. When I hit the sidewalk, I passed out. The police and ambulance were called. The Catholic Father visited me at the emergency room and calmed me down. He talked me out of filing charges on the woman, speaking to me about forgiveness and mercy. I was allowed to go home for the night.

A few days later, December 5, 1981, my labor started at five o'clock in the morning. Sanh took me to the hospital, but about one o'clock that afternoon, he had to leave for work. He did not have vacation days or sick leave so I was left alone in my labor. Carolyn arrived at 9:30 that night. I had no one with me to share the joy of the birth of my first child. She was the most beautiful baby. Sanh and I were so happy to be parents. Sanh was a wonderful father. He mixed Carolyn's milk before he went to work, making five bottles each morning.

Through the assistance of my priest, I eventually returned to work at the meat plant's cafeteria. However I became pregnant with my second child, and when the boss realized it, I was again dismissed. Fortunately, by now, Sanh had been at the job long enough to have insurance coverage for the new baby.

When my first son, Travis, was born on May 27, 1983, Sanh had to stay home with two-year old Carolyn while I went to the hospital with the Korean Baptist pastor. Sanh arrived at the hospital later that morning when he was able to find someone to stay with Carolyn. Travis was much easier to deliver than Carolyn. He arrived after only about three hours of me arriving at the hospital.

When I brought Travis home, his sister was required to help me care for him. I had returned to work at Levi Straus sewing jeans. I worked the night shift while Sanh worked the day shift at his job. That way we were able to switch out caring for the children. I would try to sleep for a few hours when I arrived home each morning. I would get Carolyn her breakfast and then leave her to take care of Travis. Even though she was only two, Carolyn was able to get the milk out of the refrigerator and feed him. I was determined that my daughter would learn at a young age how to be responsible, plus I needed to sleep.

One morning Carolyn climbed on a chair, unlocked the front door, and left the apartment. I woke up and realized she was gone. I left Travis in his baby bed and went looking for her. I still did not know much English and was not sure whom to ask for help. I was scared yet mad at the same time. As I walked down the block behind my apartment, two men approached me and asked if I had lost a little girl. I understood a few words, but their hand motions made their question clear. I said "Yes," wringing my hands and nodding frantically. They told me to follow them.

They took me to a doughnut shop not too far away, and there was two-year old Carolyn, sitting in a chair wearing nothing but a dirty diaper and a popcorn box on her head as a hat, eating a doughnut and drinking a soda pop. The shop's manager had seen Carolyn walking around alone and brought her inside and fed her. I was so embarrassed that my daughter had left home unsupervised but I was relieved to see she was all right. This child of mine was becoming as independent as I was!

When she was four-years old, I made Carolyn start washing the dishes and completing other chores. In Vietnam children are taught to work at age four since most families are too poor to send their children to school. Fortunately I had been raised in a fairly wealthy family by my grandparents and did not have to work at such a young age. Instead I was allowed to attend school. But this was not Vietnam and I was no longer rich, so I was determined that my children would learn the traditional chores at a young age.

My third and last child, my son Steven, was born on February 26, 1987. By this time I knew all about labor, hospitals, and coordinating child care. I had become an expert when it came to giving birth.

In 1983 I decided I wanted to be baptized in the Catholic Church. The priest tried to talk Sanh into joining the church with me but he would not have anything to do with the Catholic religion. Sanh was a Buddhist, even though he really did not practice his religion. I thought, "His beliefs are his own, and it is not up to me to convert him; that is God's job." The day of my baptism came, and I was so excited. Sanh agreed to come to the ceremony, which made me feel special. Sister Andrea was appointed to be my godmother and stood next to me as the Father recited the words. I was not really sure what he said, but I knew those words were about me and were sent directly to God's heart. I had now been baptized by both the Baptists and the Catholics, so I felt certain I was adequately protected.

My children were raised Catholic. Sanh never objected to them attending weekly mass with me. When each of their turns came around for confirmation, Sanh attended and took photographs. My children know who God is and to turn to Him in their times of trouble.

I try to be the best mother I can. Vietnamese mothers are different than American ones. We are not as openly affectionate. I do not kiss my children goodnight, nor do I ever tell them how much I love them. Carolyn once asked me why I did not kiss her like her friends' mothers kissed their children. Since Carolyn is a child of the modern United States, she does not understand the traditional ways of my homeland. I have tried to explain to her that if I told her and her brothers how much I loved them, then my fear is they would take advantage of that love and not learn to obey me. I want my children to grow up to be strong adults and to do well in all the things they try. Most of all I have tried to teach my children to know right from wrong and to do the right thing, no matter what the consequences are. To teach them these things, I never babied my children, never made them feel too secure in themselves, or else they would not continue to try so hard.

Though Carolyn and Travis have moved far away from home to attend college, they call me regularly and seek my advice. They know I love them and that everything I do is for their benefit. Their father and I work very hard to provide them with a way of life that we were denied in Vietnam. We never had a chance to go to school, much less to attend college. We were too busy as children and young adults simply trying to survive each day. Sanh tells me that I am too hard on the children, especially Carolyn, who he says is as stubborn and independent as I.

Carolyn has told me that I have given her excellent advice about life, but that we have not had the mother-daughter relationship she desires. We have had different lives; mine has been one that my daughter has never known. I have never talked to her about my

127

experiences with life and death when I was a child. She has not heard about the violence I saw or the violence my father suffered at the hands of soldiers from both sides of the war. She has never understood why I am so rigid.

I may appear unloving, yet my devotion to my children is fierce. Perhaps the language barrier between them and me has caused some difficulties. None of my children speak Vietnamese, and my English was very poor when they were young. I wanted my children to be Americans, not Vietnamese, so I purposefully did not teach them my language.

Now that Carolyn is a young woman I realize how much heartache she had while growing up. She felt as if she could never please me. Because my temper is a reflection of my father's temper; whenever Carolyn did something I felt was wrong, I punished her unsympathetically. In turn she felt that she was a disappointment to me. However, my beautiful daughter is a source of pride for me. She and her brothers are hard workers, which, for Vietnamese parents, is a sign of successful parenting. They have excelled in school and all received college scholarships. None of them have been in trouble, and all worship God. What more can a parent ask from a child?

As for my distant family, Father tried to visit me in America in 1983. When he was leaving Vietnam he was arrested for reasons that were really never explained to us. "Does it never stop?" I wondered. He was kept in jail for a month until Sanh and I sent bail money to Mother to pay for his release. No one else ever tried to leave the country after that incident. It was good I had left when I did.

Also in 1983 I became a licensed driver. I must admit it took me several tries. I learned how to speak English more easily then driving. I passed the written test on my first try and received my permit. With my permit in hand, the moment arrived to get in the car and learn to drive.

Finally the day arrived for me to go to the Department of Public Safety and proudly show the trooper how well I drove in order to obtain my permanent license. Well, he did not think I did a good job just because I made a wide turn. "Come back and try another day," he told me. So I did. That time I stomped on the brakes too hard too many times. "OK," he said, "try again later after you practice a smoother stop maneuver." "Fine," I thought to myself, "I can do that." After a few other failed attempts, I grew increasingly nervous.

On my ninth test, I had the bad luck of getting behind a street sweeper. "Should I go around it or just show the trooper that I am a patient driver who is not in a hurry?" I wondered. I decided the safest thing to do was to follow the sweeper until I arrived at the street I need to turn on. I followed it for what seemed like hours. Finally the trooper looked over at me and said, "You can go around the sweeper since he is only driving five miles per hour. You are holding up other traffic." So of course I was politely told to try the test again on another day.

Finally, on my eleventh try the trooper said I had done well enough and could get my driver's license as long as I passed my eye test. He gave me two pieces of paper, one that said I had passed and could be given my license, and another one that said if I failed my eye test that I would need to come back after obtaining glasses. He told me to give the clerk in the license office whichever one best fit my situation. As I walked back into the building, I looked over my shoulder and saw the trooper was busy with the next applicant. I approached the clerk's window and handed her the paper that said I had passed everything. I did not want to take the chance I needed to get glasses first! I had my photograph taken and became a Texas driver. As I walked out to my car I was so excited at my accomplishment I began jumping up and down. I know people thought I was a new crazy female driver.

As the years went by I stayed busy working, raising my children, improving my English, and discovering what it meant to be an American. I attended the local junior college part-time from 1981 until 1985, studying English the first two years, and then taking business, banking, and office occupations classes the next two years. I lack only one accounting class to complete my college degree, neglecting to take the final math class. Sanh never stopped or discouraged me from accomplishing my goals.

One day it dawned on me that it was time to become an American citizen and stop being a refugee. I had been in the country for five years, the minimum amount of time required by the immigration laws before one could apply for citizenship status. I felt I was ready to try.

I sent in my application to the immigration office in Dallas, Texas, and waited anxiously to hear back. The application allowed applicants the opportunity to choose a new name once they became a citizen, so I picked the name Christy Tran. This name was easier to say than a Vietnamese name and had an American sound. "Christy" was also the name of my friend who was flattered when I asked her permission to use the same name. A few months later a letter arrived telling me I had an appointment scheduled with an immigration officer for an interview and an oral test about American history.

The day finally came for my interview and test. It was March 30, 1987. I met with an immigration officer at the U.S. Courthouse in Amarillo. I had studied hard. The test was in English and consisted of about fifteen questions. Who were the first and sixteenth Presidents? How old do you have to be to be able to be the President? How many terms can a President be in office? What are the colors of the American flag? Who was the Texas Governor? Name the branches of the American government and explain them. It seemed to go on and on, but I answered those questions. I knew what my new country was all about. I had always been a good student. I was told I had passed and promptly paid my fifty dollar application fee. A month later I attended my naturalization ceremony and was sworn in by the Federal judge, a stately looking woman. I was so proud of my accomplishment. Sanh attended my ceremony, but he had no interest in learning English or becoming a citizen. Sanh was a man who only wanted to work, support his family, and live a quiet life.

In April 1991 we finally got our own home, presented to us by the Habitat for Humanity. I had heard about the Habitat program from another Vietnamese lady. I went to the Catholic Father and asked him to help my family get approved for a home. He agreed to ask around but came back to me a few weeks later and said our family's income was too much to qualify for the program. "What?" I exclaimed. "How can that be? We only make $30,000 a year and are a family of five people." I was determined not to give up so easily.

Without telling the Father, I obtained an application from the Habitat agency, completed it, and mailed it in. We were approved. That was one of the happiest days of my life. I had my own home in my new country. I was hoping the Father would not find out I had gone behind his back and gotten the house, but unknown to me, while reviewing my application, the Habitat administrators had called him since he helped so many of the Vietnamese who settled in Amarillo and asked information about me and my family. I was so embarrassed when I found out he knew all along that I did not settle for the answer he gave me. However, he told me he was proud of me for fighting for a better life for my family. The Father came over and blessed our new home before we moved in. Sanh and I were so humbled to be homeowners. The dreams we had for our family and ourselves just kept coming true. Sanh and I celebrated our good fortune and had our first party for about a dozen friends.

I worked at the Levi Strauss Company, the place that makes the famous blue jeans, in 1983 for a few weeks, and then returned in 1992. I stayed there for five years until I had to quit because I had hurt my hands sewing the heavy fabric for all those years. The company finally closed down and moved out of town. I stayed home with my children for a while and then decided to become a hair dresser. At the junior college most people took eighteen to twenty-four months to finish, but I was determined to get through the program faster and did so within eleven months, passed the State tests, and received my license.

I worked for two years at a nationally based salon in the local mall. When I started, one of the beauticians was named Christy, which meant I had to work under a different name to avoid confusion when customers called for appointments. I chose the name "Victoria" as my professional name, even though in my personal life I was known as Christy.

I have returned to Vietnam a few times since leaving, making a trip in 1994 alone and stayed for three weeks during the New Year celebrations. Everyone in Bac Liêu came to see me. They could not believe I was the same quiet, scared girl they all had known fifteen years earlier. It was a special homecoming to see my parents, siblings, grandparents, and other family members. I did not know then, but it was to be the last time I would see my father and grandfather. Grandfather died seven months after my trip, and Father died the following year.

I returned in 1999, again by myself. Then in 2004 Sanh and I took Carolyn to meet her extended family. It was so nice to see the family embrace my daughter, and it was funny to watch them try to communicate with each other. I stayed busy translating for everyone. Even though Sanh never learned English very well, he spoke enough to communicate with his children.

On each trip back to Vietnam, I give my family money. American money is highly valued. I have to be careful not to be taken advantage of because many family members like to gamble away my hard earned money. Sadly, I have discovered some of them are ungrateful and spiteful people. They are jealous of my success and believe I am rich. They want me to keep giving them money even if they do not need it or do not spend it wisely. But I realize I am truly blessed by God. I have success that I never imagined. I believe it is my duty to return the blessings to others less fortunate, even those who are ungrateful and greedy. I know what their world is like in Vietnam. I know the difficult lives they have had and the limited opportunities. I try not to harden my heart against them. My God has shown grace and mercy to me. Am I to do any less?

My children are all on the road to American success. All received full scholarships to college, are brilliant students, motivated to succeed in life. Sanh and I are so proud of them. Carolyn received her Bachelor's degree in 2005 in Linguistics and Biology from the University of Texas in Austin and then went on to complete her nursing education as a gerontological nurse practitioner in 2010 from the University of Texas Health Science Center in Houston. She plays the piano and cello, and won several musical contests while in high school.

Travis received his Electrical Engineering degree, also from UT in 2005, and his law degree at the UT Law School in 2009. Like his sister, he is musically inclined, playing the cello and trombone in high school. Since going off to college he has also learned to play the guitar.

Steven completed his Bachelor's degree in Graphic Design in 2010 at West Texas A&M University in Canyon. He is now working on a Master's degree in Business. Steven's instrument was the viola.

My children are the reason I have persevered to overcome the obstacles that have been thrust in my path, working hard to ensure that the future Tran generations live the American dream and that they never experience the hardships I faced. I hope my family is proud of Phuong Anh, My Phuong, Nina, Christy, Victoria, of all the parts that make up the whole of me. Each name defines a chapter of my life, and I am by no means finished. God bless America.